Teaching Literacy Online

Teaching Literacy Online

Engaging, Analyzing, and Producing in Multiple Media

Rochelle L. Rodrigo
University of Arizona

Catrina Mitchum
University of Maryland Global Campus

NCTE

National Council of Teachers of English
340 N. Neil St., Suite #104, Champaign, Illinois 61820
www.ncte.org

Staff Editor: Cynthia Gomez
Manuscript Editor: Michael Ryan
Interior Design: Jenny Jensen Greenleaf
Cover Design: Adrian Morgan
Cover Image: Adrian Morgan

ISBN: 978-0-8141-0164-3 (paperback); 978-0-8141-0165-0 (epub)

Library of Congress Control Number: 2023947583

Contents

Acknowledgments

We would like to thank the reviewers and editor for their time and energy, Sallie Koenig and Angelia Giannone for insight and wordsmithing, and our families for putting up with our early mornings and late nights while working on this labor of love. We would also like to acknowledge all the fantastic teachers and students we've worked with over the years who have driven us to do this work and to continually improve our teaching and learning.

1

Using This Book

Teaching Literacy Online (*TLO*) is a practical guide for secondary and college English teachers in digital and online environments. As of the writing of this book, together we have taught online courses for 38 years. We have focused both our teaching and our scholarly careers on improving digitally mediated pedagogies. We proposed the book to the National Council of Teachers of English (NCTE) in November 2019 because we knew it needed to be written. At that time, a continuous growth of online courses was offered both at the collegiate (U.S. Department of Education, 2020) and secondary levels (Taie and Goldring, 2019). Online learning has been a specialization, *our* specialization, for decades; by 2020, however, a growing number of teachers, especially literacy educators, also accepted the need for teaching digital literacies. At the turn of the twenty-first century, scholars (e.g., Jenkins, 2006; Kamenetz, 2010), scholarly organizations (e.g., CWPA, 2008; NCTE, 2008, revised in 2019) and business and industry organizations (e.g., AT&T, 2010; Partnership for 21st Century Skills, n.d.) began to articulate key skills needed to succeed in the twenty-first century that include *information literacy* as well as the ability to *consume and compose multimedia*. These skills were already important but, with the emergence of generative artificial intelligence applications (i.e., Chat GPT) in fall 2022, became crucial.

Obviously, the worldwide outbreak of COVID-19 in spring 2020 made many more teachers realize the need for this book as well. This book is not in response to COVID-19 or ChatGPT; instead, it is a timely publication to support the growing number of English faculty who are teaching in online and other digital environments. This book is also not a general "how to teach online" book—there are a number of those floating around, and we suggest you might want to access one or two (refer to Chapter 2 for some suggestions). Instead, this book is a theoretically and scholarly based book that emphasizes sharing practical suggestions for online literacy teachers. In other words, yes, in the first part we will reference the scholarship supporting pedagogical frameworks and actions; however, our focus is on helping you with the practical steps of designing and delivering online literacy instruction. We know teaching "English" classes can include a lot of different things (e.g., reading, writing, literature, creative writing, technical writing, linguistics, film, and gender and cultural studies). The activities shared in this book are course-agnostic, meaning we present a variety of suggestions to help you and your students find, read or view, and produce digital texts in digital environments.

Like other practical "how to teach online" books, in *TLO* we include an overview of good practices and guidelines for teaching in digital environments. And, like those same books, we provide detailed suggestions that educators can implement the next day. However, the suggestions portion of the book focuses on providing literacy educators with concrete strategies for teaching in online and other digital environments, focusing on:

- the organizing and collecting of texts;
- the reading, viewing, and engaging of and with texts;
- the analysis and synthesis of information garnered from texts; and
- the production of texts in a multitude of media and modalities.

The Use of "You" in This Book

In this book, we write a lot from the first person (plural—there's two of us) as well as the second person when directing comments to the reader. However, since this book includes example assignment prompts that you might adopt and adapt, our use of *you* sometimes is directed to you, the teacher/instructor reading the book, and sometimes to the *you* of your students when reading an assignment prompt. Don't fret—the example assignment prompts are clearly labeled and visually delineated from the rest of the material.

By focusing on engaging with, analyzing, and producing texts, in *TLO* we position literacy pedagogy as the driving force when making decisions about how to teach online or with various digital applications. In short, we focus on the pedagogy of literacy learning and then share guidelines for how to translate literacy pedagogies into digital learning environments. We imagine most of these more generalizable activities could be easily adapted to more specific English courses like teaching literature or film as well as creative or technical writing.

Parts of the Book

This text is organized into three major parts:

- Part 1: Teaching Literacy Online: Some Guidelines
- Part 2: Teaching How to Find and Engage with Texts
- Part 3: Teaching the Production of Texts

Part 1 situates you in the world of online and digitally mediated instruction. Specifically, we want you to understand some of the big theoretical and scholarly tenets that drive all online teaching as well as a handful of those we think are especially important to literacy learning. You won't find theoretical underpinnings of the use of artificial intelligence in literacy learning, though we will point out some places in the practical activities where AI, should you choose to jump down the rabbit hole, could be useful.

Part 2 focuses on teaching instructors and students how to find and engage with texts. By texts, we mean both traditional alphabetic texts, like novels, articles, and blogs as well as images, videos, and audio texts, like podcasts. We think some of the exciting elements of teaching students to read texts in digital environments is the creative ways they can engage with texts by highlighting, annotating, and taking notes on and around the texts. We dedicate a good amount of time emphasizing preparation and organization in Part 2, because it can make or break doing this work in digital spaces. As you decide which texts to share with and assign to your students, we also prompt you to think about accessibility and copyright. Once you finish Part 2, we hope you will never simply assign students *to read* or *to watch* a text again; instead, you'll always assign them *to engage* with the text in meaningful and ethical ways.

In Chapters 6 and 7 of Part 2, we push the idea of engagement to include both analyzing and synthesizing different types of texts, data, and evidence.

> ***Technology Tips and Toolboxes***
>
> We can't provide a practical guide to digitally mediated literacy education without providing detailed suggestions of different types of software programs and applications. That being said, discussing specific applications immediately dates a text. For example, generative AI technologies exploded in the education world while this text was under its first review, and the first draft made no mention of interacting and teaching with those technologies.
>
> >

Throughout the book, we try to reference both more generic applications like word processing or video-editing applications and more specific suggestions. In some cases, we provide a list of specific applications you might want to use, and at other points in the book, we reference very specific applications because of the functionality they provide. We hope, however, that both the theoretical frameworks we use to guide our activity development as well as the purposes of each activity will allow future readers to understand the point and purpose of any given activity enough to swap out a defunct digital application for something that is currently available, accessible, and supported. Sometimes, we also include technology tips that are more generalized to help you understand what, how, and why something works a certain way.

We prompt you to think about students working with personal or anecdotal data as well as more traditional information from secondary sources. Again, we ask you to consider the ethical dimensions associated with analyzing and synthesizing different types of data in different environments, and we provide methods or activities to help students do that.

Part 3 focuses on having students produce digital works in and through digital environments. The majority of ideas and materials from Part 3 are just as relevant to in-person classes teaching digital project production, with a few reminders of extra steps relevant for online instruction. In Part 3, we wanted to address separately the digital production of alphabetic texts, visual texts, video and audio, and e-portfolios, along with websites and other remixes. These chapters start with a discussion of typical conventions to consider while working in those media. The chapters then discuss activities to help students select and learn relevant technologies. Finally, these chapters include suggestions for both preproduction and polishing activities.

Sections of Each Chapter

Clarifications and Considerations

Some chapters have boxes that provide specific, focused clarification. You've seen two so far in this chapter (the first discusses our use of *you* and the second articulates our approach to suggesting different applications). These are clarifications and considerations, sometimes definitions, that we deem important enough to your understanding to highlight them. In Chapters 2 and

3, we emphasize the need to consider activities through the lens of accessibility and social justice; these can be complex to apply in different situations. Some clarification and consideration boxes prompt you to examine and reflect upon the more theoretical and philosophical implications. Finally, there are some clarification and consideration boxes where we explicitly introduce notes having to do with AI technologies.

QR 1.1. *Sample Introduction to AI Activity*

Especially if you plan to incorporate AI technologies into your class, we suggest that one of your first activities be a discussion that allows you and students to explore your knowledge and expectations around AI: https://tlo.pub/AIactivity

Suggested Applications

Technology Toolbox: Technologies for This Type of Work
Example 1
Example 2
Example 3

Many chapters have other boxes that offer technology options for the types of activities that we're suggesting. Those technologies are current as of the most recent update of the book and represent the types of programs that are mentioned in the chapter but also include other potential options. We give these other options because technologies can sometimes disappear from existence (often replaced by something newer and shinier).

Links to Websites and Applications

When we use titles of specific applications, it's because the application usually has a very specific function; otherwise, we try to emphasize the purpose and functionality of tools. Each chapter contains a variety of tools that may serve the same purpose but are chosen because of other affordances of the technology. We don't recommend you use a different technology for each activity as we have; we touch on planning tech selection in Parts 2 and 3. Our goal is to give you a breadth of options that are current to the latest edition of this text. At the end of each chapter, we provide links to the websites and applications that we've mentioned. As with the suggested application boxes, these are the links and applications that existed at the time of publication.

Learning Activities

Throughout each chapter are learning activities that we've designed to help with teaching the concepts we're discussing. The learning activities are largely structured the same way. At the top of the activity boxes are the title and

Learning Activity number intended for your own navigation purposes. These numbers start with the chapter number, followed by a period, followed by the chronological order that the activity falls in within that chapter. For example, the template included in this section is titled Learning Activity 1.1, and the third activity in Chapter 5 is Learning Activity 5.3.

The next part of the learning activities you'll see is a header inside of angle bracket (e.g., <h1>). These indicate that, in the creation of these activities in your own Learning Management System (LMS), you should be applying that level of header to the bolded line it precedes. This is a practice that is necessary when considering best practices for accessibility and Universal Design for Learning (UDL), as it allows for those using a screen reader to easily navigate through an activity or document.

Intro Headers

At the top of each activity, we list "Intro Header." For every activity in an online class, we suggest you provide students with a bulleted list of specific elements to help them situate and prepare for the activity. These elements are intended to help guide student expectations (Pleitz et al., 2015) about what their experience with the activity will look like.

Purpose: You'll want to provide the purpose of the activity because it helps students to see the connections between what they've done, what you're asking them to do, and what you'll be asking them to do later. Students generally appreciate transparency in what they are being assigned. Some examples of purposes include:

- Brainstorming ideas for a paper or project and then workshopping ideas with classmates to help narrow or develop more focus.
- Collecting images to use in the upcoming presentation.
- Reading the next section of the class book. Engaging with the content to be prepared to discuss _____ during the next synchronous class period.
- Finding secondary resources for a research project.
- Reading and taking notes from the secondary resources.
- Synthesizing information across secondary resources.

Tech Tools: We suggest listing the technology tools that students will use in the activity. This is critical if you require students to work in a number of different environments or with different applications so that students can plan accordingly. For example, we've been known to require that students use applications like PowerNotes, Hypothesis, or Perusall for class reading. In the same course, we've required that they use the discussion board in the LMS for some activities and Google Docs in a shared Google Drive folder for others. With the addition of the LMS and its other functions (e.g., assignment submission, quizzes), that adds up to four separate required technologies. Even though we share this example, we always recommend streamlining tools as much as possible.

Submission Space: Especially if you have students submit work in multiple locations, you might want to list the submission location at the top of the activity. If submission guidelines are a bit more complicated, you might want to include a larger submission section in the text of the activity assignment as we discuss below. You'll see some examples of these detailed instructions across this book.

Estimated Time: First and foremost, everyone experiences time differently, and many factors can impact how long an activity takes students to complete. Including estimated times (or estimated time ranges) helps students with planning and scheduling time to complete the activity, but it's critical to articulate a few things to students:

- how you came to your time estimates,
- that *you* understand that there are a variety of factors that impact how much time an activity might take them, and
- that taking more time than is estimated to complete an assignment is not a deficit.

The first few times you do these estimates, get student feedback to see how close you are and potentially start giving a "range." We admit, including estimated time is difficult. At minimum, include the length of videos and, if you require reading, consider providing an estimated reading time based on the average reading speed for the student population you are teaching (and make sure to tell them the rate of words per minute you are using so they can adapt as needed).

Grade: We've included a number of points possible here; they are directly related to the rubrics that we list at the end of each activity. In most of our rubrics, students earn one point for completing each rubric item (see Assessment Sections below for more information about the rubrics).

Outcomes: The outcomes section is where you connect the activity to the course or module level outcomes. Many online course design evaluation rubrics want to explicitly see connections between activities and course outcomes. Sometimes we think this is overwhelming to make visible to the student (especially at the activity level); however, some evaluation rubrics require it. First, this is just more information for the student to process (and we are already prompting you to include a lot), and if you truly want to be transparent

QR 1.2. *Link to Full Course Outcomes Map*

To see different examples of outcomes matched with activities, visit the example mapping the activities across an entire course: https://tlo.pub/CourseMap

to students, avoid using jargon that we use amongst ourselves as teachers. We believe students are better served by the purpose statement above; in terms of outcomes, however, you should have some type of course map that connects course outcomes to all modules/units and learning activities. You can then choose to share that with students when appropriate (see Figure 1.1 for a snippet of an example).

After that intro header prompt, we flesh out more details for you; however, anytime you need to insert information for your students or make a decision particular to your context, we've identified these areas in red text with the words "instructor insert." In places where we highly suggest you make changes or add information, we've included "instructor suggestions" in **green text**. Finally, we have "instructor notes" in **blue text** that articulate side comments such as other things you might do and consider. Like with clarification boxes, green instructor suggestions and blue instructor notes might also include thoughts about accessibility, social justice, and AI technologies.

As far as the activity designs themselves, we've broken down activities into smaller chunks. The reason for breaking the work down in this way is twofold: 1) this format helps students break tasks down into chunks of time; and 2) we do

Module 1: Researching and Exploring a Topic				
Due Date #	**Course Outcomes**	**Module Outcomes**	**Assignments**	**Purpose of the Assignments**
2	Goal 1 Goal 2 Goal 4 Goal 5	1D. Explain how and why a text's audiences, purposes, and contexts influence rhetorical options. 1E. Adapt composing practices (including rhetorical choices) to a variety of audiences, purposes, and contexts. 2C. Use a variety of research methods, including primary and/or secondary research, for purposes of inquiry. 2D. Evaluate the quality, appropriateness, and credibility of sources. 2E. Synthesize research findings to develop arguments. 4E. Evaluate and act on peer and instructor feedback to revise their texts. 5A. Narrate their processes and progress as writers throughout Foundations Writing courses. 5B. Recognize and articulate how their values, goals, and/or circumstances inform their choices as writers. 5C. Assess how writing experiences and artifacts might influence future writing situations.	DD2HW1: Research, Rhetoric, and the Disciplines (Discussion Board)	To consider the role that research and rhetoric and disciplinary differences play in writing
			DD2HW2: Explore Possible Topics (Discussion Board)	Start exploring possible topics for Project #1
			DD2HW3: What is Peer Review? Posted in Eli Review (Eli Review)	Exploring the importance and best practices of peer review
3	Goal 2 Goal 3	2C. Use a variety of research methods, including primary and/or secondary research, for purposes of inquiry. 2D. Evaluate the quality, appropriateness, and credibility of sources. 3D. Identify and effectively use variations in genre conventions within and/or across genres, including formats and/or design features.	DD3HW1: Identify a Topic & Generate and Post Research Questions and Search Terms (Discussion Board)	Identify and narrow your topic to a research question and generate search terms for Project #1

FIGURE 1.1. Snippet of a Course Outcomes Map

not want to assume that students know how to work with digital technologies, and so, we need to have more steps built in. For example, in the areas of the activities that articulate to students how to submit, you'll notice we often ask students to submit a URL. URL, or "Uniform Resource Locator," is the web address for the work that students will be sharing. Breaking the activity into small chunks allows you to more easily expand or condense the activity as well as break it up into even smaller assignments, if you need to.

We also want to explain the way that we've articulated the reading and viewing requirements and how this impacts estimated time. You might have some assignments that students need to read or view in their entirety and others that they only need to review or skim. Clearly identify this requirement for each text you assign. This will help you create better time estimates for assignments that in turn will help students determine how much time they will need to spend on an assignment. For example, you might preface lists of texts that don't need a careful read with "spend no more than x minutes and focus on X" in order to help students identify what their needs are and how to spend their time. Because of various reading speeds, when you assign text students must read in its entirety, you'll need to make sure you revisit the estimated time section. Be sure to give students advance warning that a specific reading may take longer than estimated depending on their individualized reading speed. We've included "how-to" instructions within the read/view section of our learning activities. If students already know how to use the technology, they might not need to read or view the support materials. For example, a student already knows how to use highlighters and pens while reading and annotating a hard-copy book; if they are new to annotating using a digital application, it may take them more time to learn and use the unfamiliar features. Other times, you might need students to read or view course content, technology instructions, or other materials in their entirety.

Activity Instructions

Depending on what the activity asks of students, the activity assignment instructions might include a variety of categories that start with an action verb. We've already mentioned the intro header and the reading/viewing sections, and we discuss rubrics below; other activity assignment instruction categories we include across the examples are:

Write/Add/Create: This is usually the deliverable of the activity.

Comment/Respond: For many activities, you might want students to read and respond to one another's work. Comment instructions should include at least three pieces of information:

- The number of responses they're required to write;
- The required number of comments/responses per classmate (especially if they are leaving comments in a word-processing document); and
- The specific response framework they need to use when commenting (e.g., answering specific types of questions, making specific types of suggestions).

Reflect: Many literacy studies scholars emphasize the importance of reflection as a way to improve learning (e.g., Alem, 2019; Belanoff, 2001; Yancey, 1998). Since our literacy classes often require students to construct learning e-portfolios at the end of the course, we tend to include a lot of mini-reflections associated with specific learning activities (not just major projects). As with commenting, students will appreciate detailed suggestions on exactly how they should reflect upon the activity. Some reflection frameworks you might use include:

- *Process:* What steps did a student take to complete the activity? How does this particular activity contribute to the process of a larger project? How did they overcome any challenges?
- *Rhetorical Framework:* How does this project help identify or support the various rhetorical elements required of this or a larger project (e.g., audience, purpose)?
- *Learning:* What did the student learn while doing this activity? How does this activity contribute toward learning-module or course-learning outcomes? How does the activity or what they learned connect to recent readings or lectures?
- *Technology:* What technological choices did they make during the activity? Why did they choose specific technologies? How did they find and use support for the technologies?

Submit: If you ask students to do work in multiple places or in multiple media, you likely need to provide some detailed suggestions for final submission. Elements we commonly find ourselves specifying include:

- *File Type:* For example, depending on what you want students to do next with an image, you might suggest they save their file as a .png instead of a .jpeg.

- URL: Sometimes the file students produce cannot, or you do not want it to be, downloaded. You might request that students copy and paste the URL as their form of submission.
- *File Name:* Once we started teaching online and sometimes downloaded batches of student papers, we realized we needed to remind students that although "eng101-project1" might work as a file name for them, we are collecting twenty-five files with that name. We typically suggest students include their last name in a file name. We provide suggestions like "LastName-eng101-f22-p1draft."
- *Submission Location:* Especially if we are keeping the course gradebook in the LMS, we usually ask that students submit all their work in the LMS. Sometimes we have a bunch of "assignments" in our LMS that are just repository spaces for students to submit URLs to where their work might reside elsewhere. For example, if you're working in Google Docs, this might be just a link to the doc. However, you will need to consider the functionality of your LMS. Some allow you to have textbox submissions (where students can drop a link) and some require only file submissions.
- *Submission Requirements:* Sometimes you might have specific requirements that either make the next step easier for students or make it easier for you to assess. For example, sometimes we've prompted students to include an image via copy and paste as part of their discussion board post rather than attaching the image as a separate file. Similarly, many LMS assignment areas allow for either attachments or direct entry of text in a text box.
- *Sharing Permissions:* If you have students share a URL to their submission or have them submit in a digital repository space like Google Drive or Dropbox, remind them to check sharing permissions—at the minimum, you need to see it to assess the work. If students need to see one another's work, they have to make sure the materials are shared with their classmates or the technology is set to some public or "anyone with the link can view" permission. We have managed courses in which we set up a digital repository space shared with all students at the beginning of class, and we then prompt students to always submit their work in that area. This ensures that, as long as the students submit their work in the shared file space, everyone will have access to the files.

Assessment Sections

At the bottom of some activities is a rubric list. These rubrics are completion-based and are used to gauge whether specific elements are present in a student's submission. In many instances, the rubrics closely parallel the scaffolded steps outlined in the activity instructions. These rubrics point to specific steps the activity has asked students to complete and focus on task-based specifications (Inoue, 2019; Nilson, 2014) to assess the work. If you remove tasks or add tasks, you'll want to recalculate the grade for the activity. While we only provide a few rubrics throughout, we recommend you articulate the number of points for each task students are asked to complete.

Learning Activity 1.1: Template Activity Prompt Box

<h1>Title of the Activity

<h2>Intro Header

- Purpose:
- Tech Tools:
- Submission Space:
- Estimated Labor:
- Grade:
- Outcomes:

(Instructor suggestion: If you already have activities you assign in an online course, you might want to adopt or adapt this framework.)

<h2>Read/View

<h2>Write/Add

<h2>Comment

<h2>Reflect

<h2>Submit

<h2>Rubric/Grading Criteria

(*Instructor suggestion: Ideas and frameworks that you DEFINITELY want to consider when implementing the activity.)

(*Instructor note: Tips and tricks you MIGHT want to consider when implementing.)

(*Instructor insert: Spaces where you need to add materials or instructions that are specific to your course.)

Calculating Grades

We calculated grades based on each task being worth one point because we identify the inclusion of each element as a criteria in the rubric. Alternatively, you could make each task worth two points (allowing for partial credit if you find yourself lumping elements together). For example, if you ask students to find three resources, each resource could be a single criterion (one point for each criterion equals three points), or you could lump those three resources together into a single criterion (two points for all three resources being present, one point if only 1–2 are present, and zero if none are present). Assignment points can also become more complex if you want multiple pieces of work completed per task assigned. For example, you might ask students to find three resources, and for each resource, write a full bibliographic citation, summarize the source, and briefly discuss how or why they think the source will be useful for their project. In that case, assigning a single point per activity is three sources multiplied by three points each (citation, summary, and description), making the entire amount of work equaling nine points. In online courses, we have found we usually also assign points for correct submission format (e.g., shared URL, PDF file format) as well as for specific file name (e.g., LastName-Research-Project1-ENGL307).

Just as there are a few ways to chunk tasks in the assessment of these activities, there are a few ways to indicate to students on what they will be assessed. We like to use a list-style rubric so students can use the rubric as a checklist to make sure they've included all of the tasks and elements. We refer to these as completion rubrics. For example, our secondary resource example above would look as follows:

Rubric (11 points)

- URL to shared Google Doc (1 point)
- Document named LastName-Research-Project1-ENGL307 (1 point)
- Three sources with the following information for each (3 × 3 points = 9 points)
    - Full bibliographic citation (1 point)
    - Summary of source (1 point)
    - Brief description of how the source will help with the research project (1 point)

Alternatively, you could incorporate a table that articulates the expectations and values to students. Your LMS likely allows you to link to the rubric as well, but we find students are less likely to use it as a guide if extra click steps are needed. If you elect to use a table (Figure 1.2), be sure to format the table as a table (and not as an image) and include alt tags so that those using screen readers can use and understand the table.

Criteria	Present	Not Present
Criterion 1 (example: Initial discussion post includes answer to question 1)	1	0
Criterion 2 (example: Initial discussion post includes answer to question 2)	1	0
Criterion 3 (example: Responded to one classmate with a question)	1	0

FIGURE 1.2. Sample Grading Rubric

Chapter Conclusions: Transitioning and Connecting Ideas

In the conclusion of each chapter, we make ties between what we've done in that chapter and the other chapters. We've titled these sections *Transitioning Ideas* in the hope of giving you things to take with you in the next chapter, or *Connecting Ideas*, with the purpose of articulating how what we covered in that chapter works with the other chapters.

Connecting Ideas

In this book, especially in Chapters 2 and 3, we are scholars dialoguing with, and teachers informed by, the research and theories that support good online and digitally mediated literacy instruction. That being said, this book is not explicitly adding scholarly work surrounding digitally mediated literacy instruction; instead, this text is meant to be practical. We are focused on helping literacy instructors start or improve their digitally mediated learning activities and grounding that teaching in scholarship that already exists.

Now that you have an idea of how the sections work together, we can jump down the scholarly rabbit hole (not too far, though). In the next two chapters, we establish our scholarly grounding in online literacy instruction with a focus on online and literacy scholarship in Chapter 2 and the guidelines we design by in Chapter 3. Remember that Chapter 1 is a useful reference for the *how* of the book as you work through the *why*, the *what*, and the *how*.

Websites and Applications

Dropbox: https://www.dropbox.com/
Google Docs: https://docs.google.com/
Google Drive: https://www.google.com/drive/
Hypothesis: https://web.hypothes.is/
Perusall: https://www.perusall.com/
PowerNotes: https://powernotes.com

I

Teaching Literacy Online: Some Guidelines

In Part 1, we do the work of connecting this book to the long tradition of scholarship about online and digitally mediated learning. In Chapter 2, we briefly introduce and discuss four assumptions that ground our philosophy for teaching online: curricular alignment, scaffolding, the first week, and legalities. You can find all four of these and more in other general books about teaching online. For this reason, we give a short version that covers the key takeaways applicable to us as literacy educators. In Chapter 3, we outline and discuss our three guiding principles for teaching literacy online: social presence; time and social justice; and access, accessibility, and Universal Design for Learning (UDL). You can find these guiding principles in most of the general books about teaching online; however, in Chapter 3, we emphasize and articulate how and why these are especially important for teaching literacy online.

2

Assumptions about Teaching Online

As English teachers, more often than not, we are teaching the courses everyone is required to take; therefore, things like access and accessibility are critical. And although many instructors only think of access and accessibility when teaching in digital environments, we have found that most core guidelines for best practice in teaching online, like access and accessibility, are just as relevant to teaching in-person. Being attentive to curriculum design is also just as relevant in online and in-person instruction. For example, Darby and Lang (2019), in *Small Teaching Online,* claim online instructors should "design for learning" by "surfacing backward design." Similarly, Nilson and Goodson (2017), in *Online Teaching at Its Best,* walk instructors through writing student-learning outcomes, designing assessments that measure them, and then designing learning activities to build toward the assessments. Linder's (2017) *The Blended Course Design Workbook* provides faculty with worksheets to help with these steps. All of these "how to teach online" texts emphasize basic backward curricular design (e.g., Wiggins & McTighe, 2005) that is applicable to all course design. We don't want this book to compete with the texts above. Those texts are representative of what we have sitting on our shelves; these are the types of texts we read and suggest to others who are going to teach online to read as well. We also suggest that you might get one or two of these books as references. As we've already said in Chapter 1, this book instead focuses on teaching literacies in digital environments. However, we do use Chapter 2 to outline some basic assumptions about good online teaching and learning, including curricular alignment.

Before getting too far into frameworks that guide how we design digital literacy learning experiences, as teacher scholars who have dedicated time and energy to designing digital literacy learning experiences we want to briefly touch on the assumptions that drive this book. These are assumptions about what makes good online design (curriculum alignment, scaffolding, the significance of the first week, privacy and other legal considerations), but they are also areas we assume you're either familiar with or are willing to follow our breadcrumbs to go learn more about.

Curricular Alignment (Backward Design)

Making sure your curriculum is aligned is not a requirement solely for online courses; in reality, all of your courses should have the curriculum aligned (e.g., Bain, 2004; Graff, 2011; Nilson, 2016; Richlin, 2006; Wiggins & McTighe, 2005). When we say curricular alignment, we mean that your course learning objectives need to be aligned with your module or unit objectives, as well as your assessments, materials, and activities. By alignment, we specifically mean that these should be aligned in content (you are teaching and assessing the same information or skills) as well as in level of complexity (e.g., Bloom's Taxonomy [Anderson et al., 2000]). Let's pretend we teach math. Your curriculum would be out of alignment if:

1. If you were teaching fractions and assessing on decimals (we know they are related, but they are not the same); or
2. If you were only providing practice equations to learn fractions and then were asking students to solve a scenario-based word problem in the assessment.

If we are teaching things that won't help students meet what we are measuring, then we're out of alignment.

A common misalignment in first-year college composition is instructors not teaching syntax and mechanics but then holding students accountable for them on high-stakes papers. We'd also argue that a curriculum would be unethical if an instructor only provided instructional materials and then assessed students; in other words, we'd argue that students also need to be provided with low-stakes learning activities in which they can make mistakes during the learning process without being penalized. For example, the writing instructor could make the curriculum more ethical if they

1. identified a few syntax rules they want students to know;
2. taught the rules;
3. provided students with activities to help use and learn them, plus apply the rules to the student's own writing; and
4. on high-stakes assessments, only held students accountable for the rules they were taught and had the opportunity to safely practice and learn.

Making sure that you're in alignment requires a bird's-eye view of the curriculum.

A variety of instructional design frameworks help guide teachers in developing aligned curriculum; we're big fans of Backwards Design as articulated by Wiggins and McTighe (2005) in *Understanding by Design.* Backwards Design prompts instructors to start with the course goals, specifically the student-learning outcomes (SLOs) and then to identify the assessments used to measure the specific SLOs. Then, once the instructor has identified the assessments, they articulate a list of instructional materials and low-stakes learning activities that teach and provide the opportunity to learn the required content or skills.

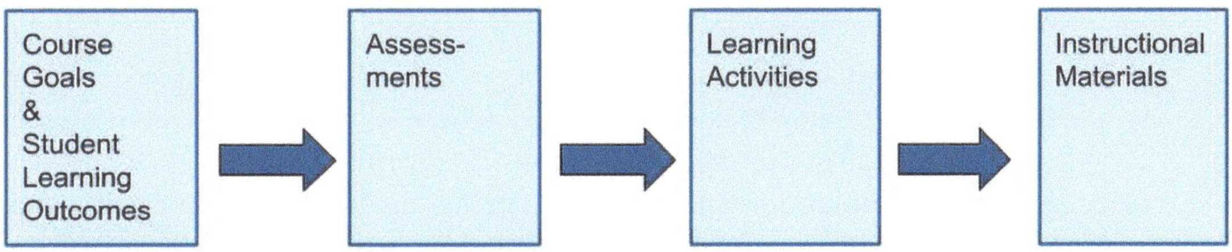

FIGURE 2.1. Backward Curriculum Design

Curricular alignment is heavily emphasized in asynchronous courses because having a well-designed curriculum helps teachers with course organization (which is critical in digital environments) as well as, if shared with the students, provides learners with the reasoning for why they are doing what is asked of them. We imagine the majority of our readers are either experienced instructors or learning to become instructors. In either case, we assume you have had instruction on, are experienced with, or have thought deeply about curricular alignment in your courses. If you need more detailed support with curriculum design, most how-to-teach-online books like Nilson's and Goodson's (2017) *Online Teaching at Its Best* and Linder's (2017) *The Blended Course Design Workbook* provide scaffolded activities to help map out course curriculum. If you're interested in the theories that help to support alignment, you might be interested in instructional design books like Reiser and Dempsey's (2018) *Trends and Issues in Instructional Design* (4th ed.) and Davidson-Shivers, Rasmussen, and Lowenthal's (2018) *Web-Based Learning: Design, Implementation, and Evaluation.*

Scaffolding

Just as we imagine the majority of our readers are likely to have previous experience designing and developing curriculum, or at least studying curriculum design in coursework, we're confident many of our readers also have experience scaffolding larger literacy assignments. In this instance, we define scaffolding as the process of breaking larger learning outcomes and student projects into smaller pieces. When scaffolded well, the smaller pieces carefully build upon one another, leading to student success. Curricular alignment, especially as described above, is a form of scaffolding. Scaffolding by breaking larger projects and complex learning into smaller pieces can also function to help students work within the zone of proximal development (ZPD). Built upon the work of Lev Vygotsky, the theory of ZPD describes student learning as happening "when students are engaging with concepts at the edge of their competence" (Saleh & Danish, 2018, p. 1840).

Using scaffolding learning and large project development, students are first introduced to content or production processes through some type of instructional material or content delivery activity (e.g., reading, video, lecture). Students then go to the next level of low-stakes learning activities in which they get the opportunity to play and experiment with the content. A lot of in-class activities and discussions as well as homework usually fall into the category of learning activities. When developing large projects, these activities usually have students building sections of the project and, sometimes, receiving feedback from others as well. The top of the scaffolded ladder is the assessment (e.g., tests, final projects, presentations), where students are tested on whether they have learned the content or skill. The smaller steps of the large project provide students the safe opportunity to practice and learn something and to revise before the higher-stakes, final project submission.

Asking students to design and develop a larger project, like a research paper or a multimedia production (e.g., video, podcast, infographic), without helping them break larger projects into smaller process-oriented steps is usually setting students up for failure (Bean & Weimer, 2011). Many larger projects can be broken down into the following scaffolded activities:

- Analyze Assignment Prompt and Models
- Identify Topic/Problem/Question
- Find and Track Secondary Sources
- Read and Evaluate Secondary Sources
- Find and Track Primary Sources
- Synthesize Ideas, Data, and Sources
- Draft
- (Peer) Review and Workshop
- Revise

- Polish
- Submit/Present
- Reflect

We're not suggesting every project includes an activity from each category above, and sometimes categories and activities overlap. For example, we strongly believe reflection should be happening throughout the entire process. However, this framework gives you an idea of the ways you can help students move from "produce this video" to a successfully completed assignment.

Again, we assume you have had experience with or instruction on scaffolding course-learning materials and major projects. As with curricular design, these are requirements of courses taught in any environment. We do, however, want to remind you of one other element that needs to be scaffolded in digitally mediated instruction: learning the technology. As administrators in a first-year writing program, we have to constantly remind ourselves and our colleagues that our students being "digital natives" is a myth (Selwyn, 2009) and that our incoming students do not necessarily know how our learning management system works. We also need to be aware of the various digital literacies we're expecting students to have—like attaching documents to emails and setting borders and headers in word-processing documents—and that not all the students know how to do these things (Dahlstrom et al., 2011). If we are going to ask students to shoot and edit videos, especially as a larger-stakes assessment project, we want to make sure to provide low-stakes opportunities to make sure students have access to the required hardware and software and know how to use it.

Designing and developing a course that is carefully scaffolded usually helps with both curricular alignment as well as course arrangement and navigation.

The First Week

In addition to the overarching design, having a well-designed introduction to the course is important for all classes independent of modality. We know we need to make sure students are aware of what the course will cover and what is expected of them. We also know the first week sets the tone for the social and emotional environment of the class as well. Online courses, however, also require precise instructions about where to get started and how the course is organized and navigated.

Setting Expectations

It is important that students understand what will be expected of them from the course. Obviously, you should share course descriptions, goals, and student-learning outcomes (usually found in syllabi as well as curriculum or course outlines). It also helps to provide a course schedule with any deadlines, especially forewarning regarding tests or other high-stakes assignments (Nilson, 2016, p. 66).

> *Course Modalities*
>
> **Face-to-face (f2f):** For many, f2f references traditional, on-the-ground, in-the-classroom courses. However, with the advancements in video meeting software, as evidenced during pandemic-induced remote instruction, f2f can now easily reference synchronous video meetings as well.
>
> **In-person**: In-person is one way to reference being in the same live, physical space.
>
> **On-the-ground**: On-the-ground is another way to reference being in the same live, physical space.
>
> **Synchronous**: Sync class meetings are when everyone meets at the same time; it could be online or on-the-ground.
>
> **Asynchronous**: Async courses are when students can work on course materials independently of the instructor and other students. Async doesn't necessarily mean online (we have a long history of async distance learning via the postal service), and it can still require deadlines (so, online students might have multiple deadlines a week).
>
> **Hybrid**: Hybrid classes mix up the modalities above. Most think of hybrid as mixing up sync and async work; however, you might also have a synchronous hybrid course where some students meet on-the-ground and others participate through video software (sometimes referred to as hyflex).

Like traditional on-the-ground, face-to-face classes, you'll also want students to know what materials they will need. An on-the-ground class might include books, notebooks, paper, and even special types of pens or pencils. Beyond books, in an online class, you might be requiring specific technologies:

- hardware processing/speed parameters (especially if students have to run large, complex applications like Adobe's InDesign or Premiere Pro);
- internet connection parameters (especially if students are required to use a synchronous video chat application like Zoom or Webex);

- specific hardware (mic, camera, etc.);
- specific software; and
- access to specific online applications.

Articulate to students that they want to have reliable access to the internet in order to be successful. We do want to acknowledge that, oftentimes, our online students don't have the access that we would prefer, and it's not something they can change. This is why the survey in Learning Activity 2.1 is so critical to student success. The answers you receive can help you assess your students' individual situations and work with them to provide solutions.

We also suggest that you make clear the time you expect the students to commit to the class (Boettcher & Conrad, 2016, pp. 49–50). Some new-to-online students think online courses do not have deadlines. If your course has deadlines, you'll want to be clear about them and what your policy is when a deadline is missed. Some new-to-online students believe online courses take less time to complete. However, the only time they are saving is the time it takes to get to campus and walk to the classroom; otherwise, the intellectual and learning time expectations are the same as face-to-face courses. And for some students, the time they gained not traveling to a campus is lost in learning how to navigate their new digital learning environments. Additionally, some new-to-online students don't consider the differences in time commitment for accelerated courses, which is increasingly common in online courses and programs. For example, instead of a regular three-credit course being offered over sixteen weeks, the online course is designed to take eight weeks and still complete the work of the same three-credit course. This would imply that the student (and teacher!) would be doing same the amount of work in half the time. Making sure students are aware of the time they need to allot for the online course commitment is critical to student success.

Finally, in addition to what you expect from them, you'll also want to articulate what they should expect from you. Nothing makes an online student panic more than not hearing back from their instructors. Help decrease your students' anxiety by providing a set of Communication & Feedback Guidelines (Boettcher & Conrad, 2016, p. 49). In short, tell students when and where they can expect to hear from you. At the beginning of a course, it's usually better to be *very* available. However, you are human, and you need to remind your students of that, especially in the age of AI. You might tell students you will check email daily Monday through Friday and once on the weekend (or not at all on the weekend). You might tell students you reserve the right to take up to 48 hours to respond because you might have to do some research, etc. We suggest you check your email daily for the first week or two. After that, you might dial back to something more reasonable. Students also want to know when you will give them feedback (even if it is only "check, saw it, you got credit") on submitted work. We usually offer something like "by the next deadline" for smaller assignments and "within 1–2 weeks" for major assignments. Turnaround time for feedback should take into account the length of the course as well as the timeline in which students need to use the feedback.

Presence and Community

QR 2.1. *Link Processing the Experiences and Expectations Survey Document*

At the beginning of the course it is important to build strong connections with the students. Responding to batches of answers will show students you are aware of their individual needs. Use these guidelines to help process the results of the Experiences and Expectations Survey: https://tlo.pub/survey

The first day and week of classes is critical for setting up the learning environment of a course. Research about successful online teaching and learning heavily emphasizes the social connection between instructors and students as well as connections students build with their peers (Barnes & Piland, 2010; Garrison et al., 1999; Moore, 1989). Most resources about teaching online stress two activities that build presence and community during the first week: introductions and netiquette guidelines. You need only search the internet for numerous examples for each.

We also suggest that you start your course with a "check-in" survey (Mitchum, Hebbard & Morris, 2021). Whether teaching on-the-ground or online, you need to know your students to create the best learning experiences for them. We currently use an "experiences and expectations" survey (Learning Activity 2.1) at the beginning of the course. The survey asks questions about their previous experiences with online courses and writing courses as well as how they'll be accessing the course and any concerns they might have. You might also include questions about students' linguistic and cultural backgrounds to better help you understand who is in your class.

We typically assign the Learning Activity 2.1, Experiences and Expectations Survey, for the first deadline in the course. Visit the digital document, Processing the Experiences and Expectations Survey, for suggestions on how to help process the answers for students who signed up for an online course (including common codes for the open-ended questions).

With smaller courses, it's easier to process all the open-ended questions yourself. If you have larger sections, or a number of smaller sections, you might want to use something like a word or phrase frequency counter to help identify trends.

Learning Activity 2.1: Experiences and Expectations Survey

<h1>Intro Header

<h2>Complete

Take the following survey: **(*Instructor insert: URL to survey)**

Potential Survey Questions

1. Name (try to design the survey to automatically collect student names and/or emails)
2. Have you taken an online college course before?

    2b. How many courses have you taken?

    2c. What were your experiences like?

3. How do you plan to access course materials?

    Your computer (desktop/laptop)

    A computer (desktop/laptop) that is owned by someone else (family member, library, etc.)

    Tablet

    Smartphone

    Other

4. Are there any issues of access to technologies that you'd like me to know about?
5. What will your internet access be like?

    I have reliable high-speed internet at home

    I have unreliable high-speed internet at home (I lose access at least once a week)

    I have reliable internet at home with speeds lower than 5mbps (it's tough to watch Netflix)

    I have unreliable internet at home with speeds lower than 5mbps (I lose access at least once a week)

    I can only access the internet through my smartphone, and I can use it as a hotspot

    I can only access the internet through my smartphone, and I cannot use it as a hotspot

    I have no way to reliably access the internet

>

6. **(*Instructor insert: questions/prompts about the specific content students will be learning in their classes, for example:**
    - **What other writing-focused classes have you taken at the college level? (Select all that apply)**
        - **Other Foundations Writing/Required Writing Course**
        - **Professional and Technical Writing Course**
        - **Advanced Writing Course**
        - **Writing Intensive Course**
        - **Other**
    - **Where and how long ago did you take those classes? What was your experience in these writing courses?**
    - **How would you describe yourself as a writer?**
    - **What is your greatest strength as a writer? (Try to think expansively about yourself as a writer here—not just academic and professional writing but also personal, creative, and social media writing.) What specific aspect(s) of your writing and/or writing process do you want to improve?)**
7. How much time do you expect to spend on coursework for this class?

    1–5 hours a week

    6–10 hours a week

    10–15 hours a week

    16+ hours a week
8. What questions or concerns do you have? Is there anything else you'd like me to know?

<h2>Rubric/Grading Criteria

Completed the majority of the questions.

Don't stop checking in with students after the beginning of the course. Check-ins don't need to be complicated. You can ask them to answer two basic questions:

- How are you doing right now?
- What do you need to be more successful with this class?

If you do anonymous check-ins, you are more likely to get honest answers, and you can provide themed feedback in batches to the classes (probably through announcements). You might provide them the option to share their names so you can provide targeted feedback and support. You could even build these check-ins as reflective parts of the course.

When assigning getting-started or check-in surveys, make sure you read and respond to the results. Students took the time to give you the information—you need to listen and respond in order to both create and maintain the feeling of support and community necessary for student success.

Organization and Navigation

Not that organization and navigation is not heavily required in other teaching environments; however, online, especially in asynchronous courses where students will be responsible for navigating the course by themselves, clear organization and just-in-time navigational support is critical. The 7th edition of the Quality Matters (2023) online course design rubric dedicates an entire General Standard, with nine specific standards, to getting started; the very first emphasizes organization and navigation. We agree with the Quality Matters rubric that there needs to be a clear "Start Here" element in the course. Ideally, any getting-started material external to the course environment, like a "welcome" email from the instructor or institution, should provide students with instructions to access your course environment. Whatever the first landing page in your individual course environment, you need some kind of obvious support for getting started.

In this case, we do have a more didactic checklist for helping students getting started and learning the navigation and organization patterns of the course. We suggest that instructors:

- have a "welcome" announcement posted in the class that includes a screencast video to give a quick tour of the course;
- send the same "welcome" announcement to the students via email or other official communication channels; and
- in the area of the course where students navigate through the class, make sure there is a clear "START HERE" (this may be the one place you can use all caps and "yell" in your course) toward the top of the page. If your LMS accommodates it, it should be the first point of entry in your course.

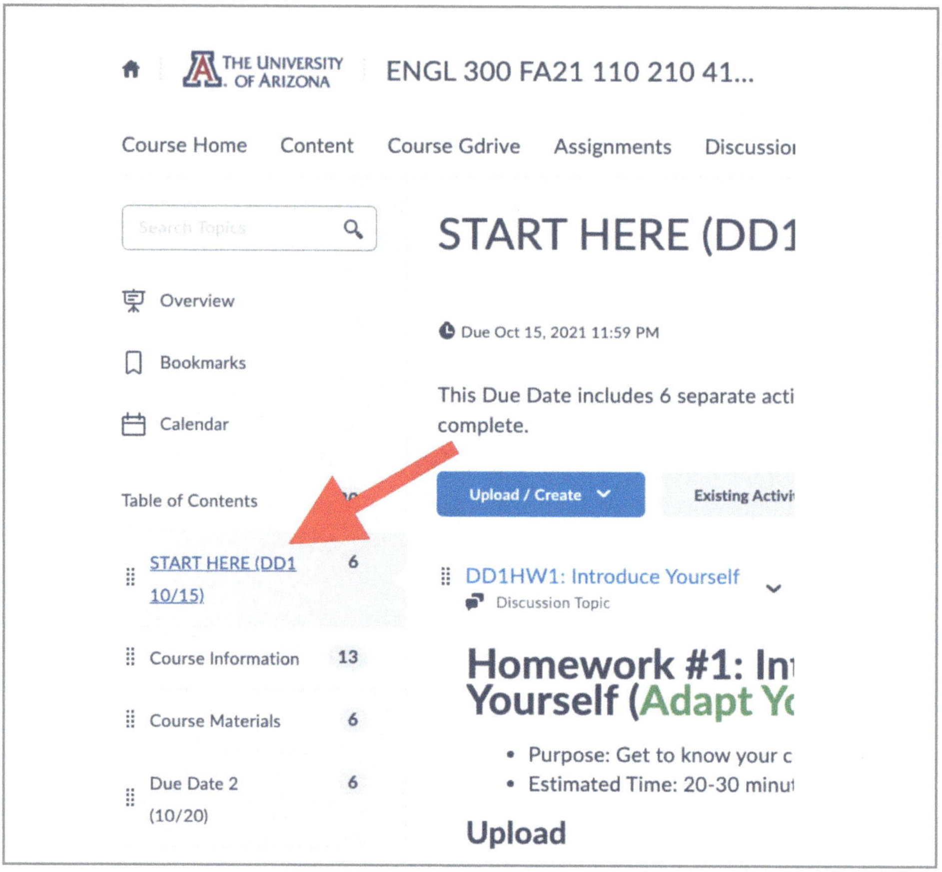

FIGURE 2.2. Emphasizing "Start Here" in Online Course Design

We suggest that the "course tour" video be short and only include enough information to get them to the "START HERE" section. Then, in that "START HERE" section, include more *short* videos to provide more detailed explanations of how the course is organized and how to do basic tasks like post in the discussion board or upload a document when submitting an assignment. Although it may be tempting to try to show students how to do all of these in one long video at the beginning of the class, they are much more likely to learn from the videos if they are short and just-in-time. Therefore, don't share or assign the video on how to upload a document until they need to upload a document. There's also no reason to recreate the wheel. If your institution has "how to post in the discussion board" resources, include them in your course before students are required to post to the discussion board.

> ***Technology Tip: Screencast Videos***
>
> Besides the tips of "keep it short" (discussed directly above) and "caption it" (discussed in Chapter 3), screencast videos have a few other formal elements you might want to consider. First, be sure you carefully articulate what your cursor is doing on the screen; for example, do not say "click here"; instead, say "go to the upper-right-hand corner and click the blue share button." In short, do not expect your viewer to easily track the movement of your cursor on the screen. Screencast videos are a fabulous place to develop social presence (Chapter 3); many include the ability to record your headshot while talking through the video (and can usually place it as a small screen within the screen). Although we suggest you practice before recording, accidents happen, and students seeing your resilience and troubleshooting not only makes you human, it also helps them understand that working through techno-glitches is normal.

If you would like more specific ideas on how to organize your first week, most how-to-teach-online books like *The Online Teaching Survival Guide* (Boettcher & Conrad, 2016) and *Online Teaching at Its Best* (Nilson & Goodson, 2017) have sections, if not whole chapters, dedicated to the "getting started" portion of an online course.

Legalities

Like the other topics in this chapter, the legal issues associated with privacy, accessibility, and copyright are not particular to the online teaching modality. However, they impact teaching in different ways when you're working in digital spaces. Privacy is harder to protect, accessibility can be more difficult (or easier) to provide, and copyright laws can be easier to break.

As they relate to particular guidelines when teaching literacy online, accessibility and copyright will be covered in Chapter 3 and Chapter 4, respectively. Privacy, though, is of underlying importance to every aspect of teaching and learning online. Most of us are guilty of accepting the terms and conditions for the use of digital applications without reading them thoroughly, and when we ask our students to sign up for technologies, we need to be aware of and inform them of what privacy rights are being "given away" by using a particular technology.

Family Educational Rights and Privacy Act (FERPA) is "a federal law that protects the privacy of student education records. The law applies to all schools that receive funds under an applicable program of the U.S. Department of Education" (U.S. Department of Education, 2021). For the past two decades, instruction at all levels has slowly been inundated with different learning technologies that then have access to student work and, depending upon the interpretation, possibly "student educational records." When an educational technology is adopted at an institutional level, in theory, a legal entity or team vets the contract to ensure FERPA will not be violated. However, just as when instructors close their classroom doors and engage students in activities that administrators may not know about (e.g., screening a copyrighted film), many individual instructors also adopt and require students to use technologies not previously vetted by a legal entity and ones that may not necessarily follow FERPA. In other words, instructors may be requiring students to use a technological application that gives the technology company access to student educational records. Considering the average length of adoption and privacy statements provided by various technology companies, it is not surprising that most faculty, and probably their students, do not closely read the statements.

Active learning in online courses often takes advantage of, and many times requires, third-party web tools and applications (Purdy, 2010; Rodrigo, 2013; Sorapure, 2010), but do we know if or how those technologies impact students' digital footprints? How are the various digital applications that students use in online courses protecting students' privacy and other data? As an instructor, you may feel like FERPA is a static federal policy protecting students; however, it is actually an ever-evolving policy with many changes made in the past decade, especially in the name of learning analytics (Fuller, 2017). Although privacy policies should help the user understand the statutory, self-regulatory, or contractual "obligations to which the organization is subject" (Hintze, 2017) and to warn users that companies may collect and use specific user data (Tschantz et al., 2012), some research suggests that privacy policies are often long and difficult to read (Sumeeth et al., 2010), and are intentionally designed to prevent readers from understanding what data is collected and used (Lindh & Nolin, 2016; Markel, 2005). Complex privacy policies combined with faculty and students who are too busy to read them privilege the technology companies in current scenarios of faculty and student adoption. One reason to limit your students' technology use to institutionally vetted technologies is because they have been checked for legal issues around privacy and accessibility.

In short, this is a reminder that you, as instructors, should be carefully reading the user and privacy statements with all the technologies you ask students to adopt. Specifically, you should be looking for:

- What information is collected about or from the users?
- Why are they collecting it? What do they say they are doing with it?
- Who owns the data?
- If users want to cancel their account or restrict access to their data, how do they do so? What happens to their data once they've canceled the account?
- Do other third-party applications have access to users' information and data? How and why?

If you are working with more mature students, it might benefit them to take responsibility for reading these statements as well; consider using some of the reading, annotating, and analyzing strategies presented in Chapter 5 to help students engage with complicated user agreements.

Transitioning Ideas

The main reminder about teaching online is that it is still teaching, and the vast majority of the strategies for teaching online well are the same for teaching well in any learning environment. Although we could write plenty more about the importance of and how we think you should manage curricular alignment, scaffolding and sequencing, first-week activities, and privacy, these are all topics that you can easily read more about in the resources that already exist about effective teaching (both on- and offline).

Websites and Applications

Adobe InDesign: https://www.adobe.com/products/indesign.html
Adobe Premiere Pro: https://www.adobe.com/products/premiere.html
Phrase Frequency Counter: http://www.writewords.org.uk/phrase_count.asp
Word Frequency Counter: http://www.writewords.org.uk/word_count.asp

3

Guiding Principles for Teaching Literacies Online

In direct contrast to what the title of this chapter implies, the guidelines below aren't exhaustive or specific to teaching English online, and they can be applied to all modalities of teaching. However, we wanted to focus on these areas because they drive the practical suggestions in this book, and they are core to the critical, ethical, and pedagogically sound teaching of literacy in digital spaces. We identify social presence as a guiding principle in teaching online literacy because online courses require us to be more purposeful in creating the social presence that is often automatic in a face-to-face setting. Our additional guiding principles of time and social justice as underlying concerns for teaching literacy online are of critical importance because online students are often short on time. In most cases, this is because they have other (often more important) responsibilities. Finally, access and accessibility are core guiding principles to any teaching situation, but they are particularly important in an online environment because there are multiple potential elements that could cause the course to be inaccessible if we were not designing universally. This chapter is scholarship-heavy in order to ground the work we're doing in this book. To help, we include clarification boxes throughout with some jargon jailbreaking.

Social Presence

Social presence, which is the creation and maintenance of a social identity, is one of three elements, including cognitive presence and teaching presence, found in the Community of Inquiry (CoI) trifecta (see Figure 3.1; Garrison et al., 1999). We start with social presence because it's student-centered and something both teachers and students construct in online learning spaces. We acknowledge that literate acts are inherently social acts where readers and writers communicate through a socially constructed networking of meaning making. English teachers and students need to be dialoguing with one another to continuously reconstruct meaning-making processes as part of literacy learning processes.

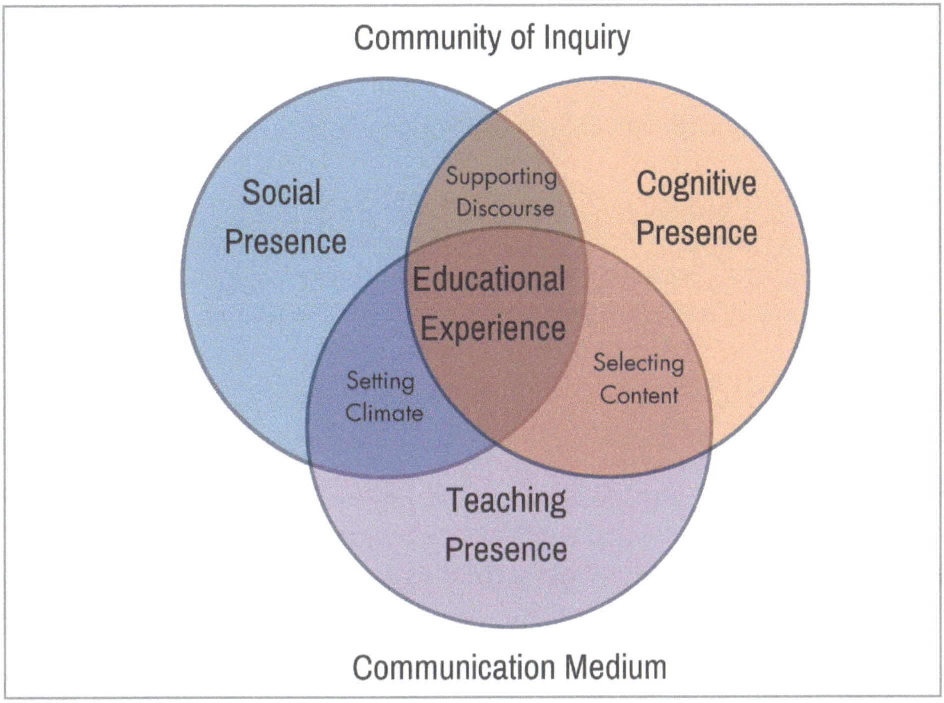

FIGURE 3.1. Venn Diagram Representing the Community of Inquiry Model from Garrison, Anderson, and Archer (1999)

In online courses, student-centered design and engagement are critical to providing space for students to create social presence. The goal of the CoI framework is to create a community of learners because it increases engagement. In this book, we're solely focusing on social presence and teacher presence. In a literacy classroom, cognitive presence often materializes as metacognitive and reflective learning activities; we didn't include it in the guidelines for teaching literacy online because it's something we assume you're already doing as literacy educators, regardless of the learning environment.

Defining Engagement

Social presence and teaching presence are important because they are negotiations and engagement between the students, the instructor, and the content. Other scholars push beyond the CoI framework by also suggesting engagement with the technologies. Engagement can be defined as "the student's psychological investment in and effort directed toward learning, understanding, or mastering the knowledge, skills, or crafts that academic work is intended to promote" (Newmann et al., 1992, p. 12).

We use "engagement," both student and instructor, as a starting point for our guidelines for teaching English online because of the student-centered approach that is necessary to teaching online.

Student Engagement

Student engagement is critical for student success. Engagement impacts students' feeling of belonging and of community (Arbaugh, 2010; Berry, 2017; Pike et al., 2010), which impacts retention (Bean & Metzner, 1985; Boston et al., 2009; Tinto, 1975;) and student success in online courses (Dietz-Uhler et al., 2007; Gaytan, 2013). Student engagement includes students' engagement with content, their teachers, other students, and technology.

- **Student-instructor**: Student-instructor engagement relies on both the design and delivery of the course. The course should be designed so that there are opportunities for the instructor to create a presence as a real person, but the instructor also needs to actively create a variety of personas in order to create a space for engagement with students (Chickering & Gamson, 1987; Grillo & Leist, 2013; Herbert, 2006; Morris & Finnegan, 2009; Nichols, 2010; Roberts & Styron, 2006). We briefly discuss more about instructor engagement and personas below.
- **Student-student**: Student-student engagement also requires good design and delivery techniques. Student-student learning activities should be designed so that students are working to create a community and want to be engaged with that community. Instructors need to encourage this creation of social presence while the course is being delivered (Dawson, 2006; Joksimovic et al., 2015; Peacock & Cowan, 2019; Phirangee et al., 2016; Shea et al., 2006; Stranach, 2017). Many of the activities we share in Chapters 4–11 either explicitly prompt student-student engagement or provide opportunities when you can add a student-student element to the assignment.
- **Student-content:** Student-content engagement requires the design of activities that allow for the understanding and application of the content in the course (Fatma & Er, 2016). Common active learning assignments designed to engage with content include reading learning materials and applying those readings to a specific task as well as actively reading and interacting with specific learning materials. The majority of the activity suggestions we provide in Chapters 4–11 fall into this category.

- **Student-technology:** Student-technology engagement requires the careful scaffolding and critical inquiry of the technologies that students will use in the course. This includes the "invisible" required technologies such as the Learning Management System (LMS) or word-processing software as well as the technologies students may elect to use in order to complete the course assignments (Darby & Lang 2019; Howard et al., 2016). Throughout this text, we repeatedly model ways you might build in learn-the-technology activities in specific assignments.

To help students build and refine a social presence, each of these engagement areas needs to be well developed in order for students to have the best chance of success in distance courses (Garrison et al., 1999). Students who perceive strong social presence, human connection, and a supportive environment report higher course satisfaction (Richardson et al., 2017; Swan & Shih, 2005), receive higher grades (d'Alessio et al., 2019; Joksimovic et al., 2015), and report an increased sense of belonging to a community (Rourke et al., 1999).

> ***Design versus Delivery***
>
> Even if you are teaching a course that you designed, we argue there is a distinct difference between the work done in the design of the course, or the things you do to plan out how the course will run, and the delivery of the course, or the way in which it is facilitated and run. For example, you design an introduction discussion board assignment and you deliver it by engaging with the students as they post responses.

We, as instructors, play an integral role in the development of social presence (Joksimovic et al., 2015; Phirangee et al., 2016; Shea et al., 2006) through our design and delivery of our online courses. Facilitating supportive student-student interactions (Dawson, 2006), collaboration (Stranach, 2017), and peer feedback and perspective-sharing (Peacock & Cowan, 2019) is essential to developing social presence and a sense of community. To encourage student-student exchange and cooperation online, some things we've done in the past are:

- use the rubric, announcements, and models to provide clear expectations for discussion participation;
- model initial discussion posts for some discussions (like the introductions and the first few discussion assignments);

- provide information and examples for working well together when assigned group work; and
- remind students to ask and answer questions in the open Q&A discussion board area.

Trust and interpersonal relationships are central components of social presence (Garrison et al., 1999). Strong student-student relationships provide incentive to interact with one another in meaningful ways (Whiteside, 2015) and to develop a sense of belonging (Peacock & Cowan, 2019) or shared identity (Rogers & Lea, 2005). It's important to recognize that the goal here is for students to view themselves as contributors working toward the same goal (Stewart et al., 2021). To encourage students to trust and be open with one another and the instructor, we have:

- encouraged students to reach out to each other;
- reminded students about course netiquette;
- in some early discussion forums, modeled engaged and considerate discussion replies by encouraging, probing, questioning, summarizing, etc.; and
- referred students to each other's responses and work as examples.

All of these suggestions attempt to develop an environment where we can assign students to work with one another in socially and cognitively productive ways.

Creating space for students to engage with us and each other is important for teaching in any modality, for any discipline. In literacy education, we tend to lean toward pedagogies that incorporate these types of engagement; however, the online element requires those spaces to look, feel, and act differently. Improving online engagement and translating in-person to online are not things we cover here, as there are many other resources out there that provide lots of ideas. We mention the need for engagement because it is a grounding principle for us and is built into the activities throughout this book. We are suggesting that because online literacy instruction involves digital texts and technologies, the affordances and constraints of these digital environments impact possibilities for engagement with one another and the content.

Collaborative Applications

If engagement is key, then the technologies in which students learn and work must help facilitate engagement. Students may miss key elements if they're only highlighting, annotating (Chapter 6), and taking notes (Chapter 7) individually. Prompting students to read and comment on one another's reading and writing facilitates deeper understanding and learning. The vast majority of digital reading, highlighting, annotating, note taking, and writing applications allow users to invite others to at least see, if not comment on, the text. When selecting applications, consider whether or not students can share their work with other members of the class.

Most of the time, we believe students benefit from seeing one another's work. Given everything we just claimed above, we also find that students benefit from doing their first round of reading, thinking, and analyzing on their own. In other words, don't forget students might need individual thinking time before sharing with others for engaged learning. Providing students with individualized thinking time is the premise that the popular Think-Pair-Share active-learning strategy is based upon.

Instructor Engagement

As instructors, we craft teaching personas in the classroom. Some characteristics of our teaching persona develop because of carefully selected choices and others because of who we are. What you wear, talk about before and after class, convey through the stickers on your laptop or your travel mug of choice, all say something about you as a human and thereby show your students that you are human with interests and hobbies and a life (Meyer et al., 2009).

Instructor Personas

A persona is a character sketch, and the following characteristics are all pieces of an online teaching persona.

Knowledgeable and Reliable: Do you have the ethos and authority to teach this course and its content? You might show this in introductions or when sharing anecdotes when teaching specific pieces of content.

Engaged Facilitator: Especially in asynchronous online courses, students want to know you are responding to them as individuals. Do you engage with their specific ideas and examples?

Involved Supporter: Students want to know that you are invested in their success. Consider trying to connect course content to their priorities or future goals.

Personable: Are you a humane human? Do you acknowledge their humanity, especially their lives outside the scope of the course?

Online teaching can start to erase those details. Don't let it. One way to build presence is by making sure your students see you as a human and don't think you are just a robot grader on the other side of the machine, especially now with prevalent use of AI-response technologies (Lehman & Conceição, 2010; Meyer et al., 2009).

One of the core theories used to discuss distance education is the concept of transactional distance. It acknowledges there is both a physical and psychological connection between instructor and student (Moore, 1989; Moore, 2019). For a lot of students, an increase in physical distance contributes to a decrease in psychological connection. In online learning, instructors need to work hard to remind all students that they are present and invested in the student's success. Students who perceive strong social presence, human connection, and a supportive environment report higher course satisfaction (Richardson et al., 2017; Swan & Shih, 2005), receive higher grades (d'Alessio et al., 2019; Joksimovic et al., 2015), and report an increased sense of belonging to a community (Rourke et al., 1999).

Here are some ways we construct human and humane or caring personas, and you might adapt or adopt these based on the specific group of students you are currently teaching:

- respond to every student's introduction post (this is the only discussion board-style assignment that we suggest replying to every post);
- share both professional and personal details about yourself in your introductory post (Catrina always shares that she's a military spouse and a parent; Shelley usually talks about her St. Bernard and cats);
- make weekly announcements and videos engaging with submissions of this particular group of students;
- don't edit out "mistakes" in videos (especially disruptions by our kids and animals);
- occasionally use personal anecdotes when making announcements or in micro-lectures;
- try using memes and gifs in announcements (no matter how uncool they are); and
- let students know when things are running late and why (e.g., kids at home, internet down, unexpected life events).

Especially if they're managing increased stress or anxiety because they are not regularly meeting in person with an instructor, students want to know that you are human and want you to understand they are human as well.

Time and Social Justice

The concern about time in general is not the only social justice concern in online literacy learning, but to us, time and social justice are intricately connected. Time is relative. It's not a new notion, and we're certainly not the first to have said it, but the relativity of time is important in online courses. Here we take up Barbara Adam's (2004) definition of clock time as *imposed* time. Clock time has become the type of time by which we're all expected to operate; however, it's important to understand that time is also cultural (Levine, 1997), experiential (Carillo, 2021; Price, 2011; Wittmann, 2017; Wood, 2017), and embodied (Grosz, 1994; Arslanova et al., 2023; Sadeghi et al., 2023). For example, we work well together, but we work better together when Catrina is in a time zone that is ahead of Shelley because Catrina is a night owl and Shelley is a lark. How we perceive clock time passing (Adams, 2004), how we each experience time (Carillo, 2021; Price, 2011), and how our circumstances (Whittman, 2017) and bodily experiences (Grosz, 1994; Arslanova et al., 2023; Sadeghi et al., 2023) impact those perceptions are critical to online students. These concepts about time are particularly critical to online students in literacy courses. When considering our content (typically alphabetic text based), we need to consider variations in reading speeds and how that might impact not only how much clock time but also how much perceived time doing a reading might take our students (Wittmann, 2017; Carillo, 2021). We need to consider that previous experiences with both the content and the learning processes (e.g., reading, lecturing, certain types of activities and assignments) all impact how a student experiences the act of doing them again.

Time Management

The online student population struggles with time (Song et al., 2004; Wandler & Imbriale, 2017). Some students are short on time as a resource, and others may need more direct instruction in managing their time (e.g., Globokar, 2012). Online students are usually self-selecting to take online courses for a reason. Online students who are not traditionally college-aged are more likely to work, usually full-time jobs, to be responsible for the care of others (children, parents, siblings, a partner), and are less likely to be able to compromise on the time spent on those two pieces of their lives (Nash, 2005). Online secondary students are often taking online courses to start working on their college degree (Matuga, 2009) or because attending online school gives them affordances that attending in-person does not (Lewis et al., 2014). Some students enroll in online courses because their bodies don't do well in the process of attending classes on the ground (due to mobility, neurodiversity, etc.). All of these students elect to take online courses for a variety of reasons, but flexibility in scheduling is often a top concern because of responsibilities and constraints that pull on these students' time (Moore et al, 2003) and can also be a problem without useful strategies (van der Meer et al, 2010). When forced to choose between self-care, others they care for (or their job that feeds their families), and school, they do (and should) be prioritizing the lives they have outside of school. Any time you are working or learning from home, it takes concerted effort to plan and stay on task. Our online student population is often the most vulnerable and most at-risk (Moore et al, 2003; Nichols, 2010; Pontes et al, 2010), which means we need to consider our approaches to timeliness in online courses as a question of social justice.

Online students often articulate that they need to be able to manage their time (van der Meer et al, 2010; Song et al, 2003), yet articulating how to enact that management is more difficult (van der Meer et al, 2010). While critiquing certain implementations of labor-based grading contracts, Ellen Carillo argues, "while students may be willing to participate, time is a luxury that not all students have" (2021, p. 15). In order to have a socially just online course, building in time-management strategies with options for students (such as multiple deadlines, the articulation of critical versus helpful activities, and the scaffolding we mentioned in Chapter 2) is critical. One aspect of those time-management strategies is acknowledging that your students are constantly distracted by other priorities. The act of going to school and sitting in a classroom can help a student temporarily draw a line between their outside life, distractions, and responsibilities and the focus they want to give to their class. Whether students have work and caregiver responsibilities or just that they are trying to do this work at home, they are in an environment that reminds them of things they should be doing (e.g., washing dishes, cleaning laundry, doing yard work) or would rather be doing (e.g., watching TV, petting the cat, catching up on sleep). When students use the time for class that they would otherwise use cooking dinner, driving to work, or listening to a podcast, their attention is split from the start. Even using the same device used for gaming, social media, and online shopping for school blurs the environmental boundaries between life and learning. On the one hand, that can be good to help students see the connection between what they are learning and the rest of their daily activities. On the other hand, it's a distraction that potentially impacts time management, focus, and, therefore, learning. Although Cathy Davidson (2011) reminds us that we are always already distracted, we can also prompt students to pay attention to *how* they pay attention and make connections while and across multitasking activities.

To acknowledge students' finite amount of time as a resource and a critical consideration for socially just education and assessment, we suggest that you:

- build in time-management activities;
- provide engagement choices by articulating the activities that are "critical," "important," "non-critical but useful if struggling with. . ." so students can make choices;
- be empathetic and adapt deadlines without grading for timeliness as needed;
- break assignments into small chunks that they can do in one sitting (which also supports the need to scaffold);
- develop metacognitive, reflective activities that help students be more aware of their time, attention, and connections across activities both inside and outside of their coursework; and
- prompt students to refocus/recenter their bodies as they switch tasks.

First, we suggest prompting students with explicit time-management activities to help them set aside time for the course and then periodically checking in to see if that plan is working. You might share with students various strategies and digital applications for calendaring, developing to-do lists, and tracking time. All of these time-management activities are not useful if you don't have students reflect upon what works, what doesn't work, and how that changes over time.

As an instructor, you can build in make-up time slots. You might allow students to make up all work in a unit prior to the final unit test or deadline. You might have Monday, Wednesday, and Friday deadlines and let students know they can always make up the work from a week until Sunday at 11:59 p.m. For years, we have allowed our online writing students to make up all work until the end of the term, except drafts and peer reviews. (We explain that classmates need those to do their work on time.) We emphatically remind everyone when a hard deadline is approaching, and we can sometimes give a one-day grace period, depending on the assignment and required turnaround time for others. One of the most important aspects of this approach is that we don't punish students for turning in late work. We reserve the right to in the syllabus, but timeliness should not be used as a metric in online classes that are socially just. Grading for timeliness and taking off points for being late says to our already strapped-for-time students and students who are still learning to manage time, "We don't care about you and your learning and prioritizing." For us, when research shows that the "traditional" college student is a shrinking minority (Deil-Amen, 2011), penalizing students for late work is unethical. From what we understand about the reasons for the "typical" secondary student taking online classes (Lewis et al., 2014), the strain on their time is just as contentious. In our courses, we use rubrics built for individual assignments that have discrete pieces of the assignment listed as criteria and whether or not they're present, without accounting for timeliness, in order to manage a socially just assessment system. To be clear, we do have specific dates by which students need to complete work; the course is not self-paced.

Finally, breaking assignments into small chunks allows extremely busy students (and teachers) to fit in work for class when they can. If it is something that can be completed in 15–30 minutes, they can do one or two activities during a lunch break. Similarly, scaffolding large projects by breaking them into pieces means students are less likely to try to complete the entire project the day it is due.

The key is flexibility and choice in order to help students gain agency over their time and learning, and whatever you choose, you must be sure to communicate it clearly with your students.

Communicating Your Time Management to Students

We know that an instructor's social presence is a key indicator of student success in digital learning environments and that not being present is not supporting student learning. Making sure students know when, where, and how you will provide feedback and grades for homework, projects, exams, and the entire course and adhering to what you communicate is paramount for students being able to manage their time as well. Whatever the circumstances, just make sure you communicate with students and then stick to it. For different assignments, as well as the entire course, students would appreciate knowing:

- the type of feedback to expect from you;
- when to expect the feedback;
- where to find the feedback;
- how to contact you with any questions or concerns; and
- when you will respond.

Planning, articulating, and sticking to your own time management strategies can help reduce student stress.

When teaching online (or with technology in general), we expect the technology to fail. Links are broken, files are empty, files didn't upload, webpages didn't publish, things were submitted to the wrong place, etc. Make sure you and your students are prepared to act! Help students reduce last-minute, error-induced stress by proactively planning for problems. Once students submit a final online, they might be inclined to check your class off the list. It's important to articulate that **$#!^ happens** and what your plan is if a submission snafu occurs. For example, you can tell students, "If I can't find your work, I'm going to contact you within 24 hours (or two days or the following Monday) after the final submission is due, so check your email!" This means that:

1. You need to tell students to make sure to check their emails (or other communication lines) 24 hours after the final submission—we suggest putting this in final assignment or exam prompts, course announcements, and any other reminder venue; and
2. You need to confirm that you can access each student's submission within 24 hours after submission.

This doesn't mean you must assess the work within that time frame; you just need to confirm that it was submitted and that you are able to access the work for assessment purposes. Some LMSs provide submission confirmation. However, depending on the assignment, the work may be submitted, but you are still unable to open and view the file. Planning ahead for techno-glitches will save time and energy when things don't work or are missing.

You do need to be present and active in the course, but often the balance you find for yourself and managing your own time can benefit your students as well. It's about finding harmony. For example:

- You can set up office hours by appointment instead of sitting and waiting for students to show up. This both protects your time and allows online students the flexibility they need in their day. We have access to Google Calendar and can set up appointments that students can easily sign up for as well through their own Google accounts. This also allows students to select the medium: phone, chats in a preferred chat app, or Zoom/ other video conferencing. Calendly is another scheduling application we enjoy, but it does have limitations with the free version.
- If you are continually getting the same questions or concerns via email, consider setting up a questions discussion board for students (see Learning Activity 3.1) or keep an FAQ list that you can post with the note, "Please take a look in this place and let me know if you have further questions." This will help students get answers to their questions faster, if their questions have already been asked.

Most important, whatever parameters you set need to be clearly communicated to your students. They need to know when and how to get in touch with you and when and how they'll receive a response. Remember, you need to take care of yourself before you can adequately take care of anyone else.

Learning Activity 3.1: Q&A Anonymous Discussion Board

<h1>Intro Header

(*Instructor suggestion: When you create the instructions, encourage students to answer each other's questions, to search the web, and to subscribe to this particular discussion forum. This not only helps students continue to create a supportive community but also provides a central space for questions. You'll want to subscribe to this particular forum—or check it every day—so that you receive notification when there is a new post.)

<h2>Post

This discussion board (DB) area is where you can post questions, concerns, comments, etc. The idea is that if you have the question or concern, some of your other classmates probably have it as well.

FIGURE 3.2. Ask 3 B4 Me

If you post here, other classmates may respond more quickly than the instructor (please, do so!). You also have the ability to post anonymously, so don't be afraid to ask a question.

Unbiased Assessment

Over the last decade or so, there have been multiple calls for antiracist pedagogy (Condon & Young, 2016; Inoue, 2015; Inoue, 2019). These calls argue that we should fight against hegemonic writing standards and deficit language ideologies (Flores & Rosa, 2015; Young, 2009) that focus on White Standard English in academic writing. Part of this call has included antiracist writing assessments (Inoue, 2015; Inoue, 2017). Assessment is supposed to focus on how we measure learning. For example, in first-year college writing classes, we measure the students' ability to produce required elements of a specific genre's use in specific contexts. The question becomes: Whose ideal or standard of "appropriate" or "good" is being used to assess how well the student executes the requirements for the assigned genre and context? The argument for antiracist writing assessment is supported by a framework that argues that holding students to a standardized English in order to assign grades is not only unethical but racist. Assessing students based on the labor completed in the course is an example of antiracist writing assessment. Assessing labor allows instructors to separate assigning a grade from giving feedback. The feedback can then help students grasp concepts and improve outside of the grading scheme (Inoue, 2019).

Labor-based contracts often rely heavily on synchronous negotiation—these contracts can be difficult to enact in an online class, especially one that's accelerated or has no synchronous component (Parkes & Zimmaro, 2017). Labor-based contracts assume that labor is neutral in ways that create problematic inequities for students of varying socioeconomic classes and abilities (Carillo, 2021; Kryger & Zimmerman, 2020), and they assume it takes everyone the same amount of time, physical ability, and cognitive energy to read, write, and think. These very real concerns for specific intersectionalities of students and their struggles with time, as well as our desire to enact antiracist assessment, has led us to use what we call "completion rubrics."

We use the theoretical underpinnings of labor-based assessment and what we know of experiences and perceptions of time to create completion rubrics that aim to function in the same way: assign the institutionally required grades to getting work done and leave formative feedback to do the work of learning. Rubrics are a common assessment tool across education, and they have their affordances and constraints. Rubrics, when done well, have the affordance of providing clear and transparent grading criteria to students, which is a particularly important tenet for the Universal Design for Learning framework (CAST, 2020; Nilson & Stanny, 2015). The constraints of rubrics often lie in what they're measuring. For example, if a rubric is measuring the quality of writing based on a particular "standard" of English, then it's putting many of our BIPOC students at a disadvantage as they're trying to learn the concepts introduced in our classes (Inoue, 2017). Taking these ideas a step further, if we give students choices in how they engage in the course by articulating the critical tasks and assigning required points with helpful tasks taking on extra credit, then we're doing right, based on what we currently know, by our intersectional students. Completion rubrics are based on observable, measurable tasks instead of focusing on the quality, appropriateness, and correctness features of the writing. For example, instead of using "incorporate three appropriate sources as evidence in your argument" as a criteria, use "incorporate three scholarly or peer-reviewed sources." In other words, what is considered "quality" writing is highly contextualized, and when it becomes characterized as the "norm," it becomes biased. For us, this has resulted in working toward crafting completion rubrics that give students credit for the completion of discrete tasks. These rubrics do not count students' late work against them because of the realities of time constraints identified above. Each activity is given one point for a potential task being complete in that activity and zero points for tasks that are missing. Chapter 1 (Table 1.1) contains the template we use for each sample learning activity in this book.

As with all the guidelines we suggest, socially just curricular development and assessment are issues relevant to all literacy instruction. We hope this section prompts you to consider how time and rubric design are especially relevant as social justice issues in online literacy courses.

Access, Accessibility, and UDL

Access and accessibility are critical to student success in an online course (e.g., CAST, 2018; Novak & Thibodeau, 2016; Womack, 2017). For this text, we focus on these two particular guiding principles that are also important in our face-to-face English courses but that manifest differently online.

Access means having access to basics, like a machine to complete the online course and the internet, but also access to time and space to complete the work. However, these "basic" needs are not the only access needs we need to be concerned about. What types of machines are students using to access the course? How will that impact their experience with the materials and their success? Have we designed the course to be mobile-friendly? What support can we offer when students' internet service goes down? If we haven't considered these questions, we're doing a disservice to our most vulnerable students (Pontes et al., 2010). Having the standard and expected access to materials in order to be successful in an online course is often a socioeconomic issue, and those students who don't have what they need are often our students who have a lower socioeconomic status (Pontes et al., 2010).

Software access is another concern in online courses. This access issue is often a digital literacy concern as well (Dahlstrom et al., 2011). We cannot assume that our students are digitally literate or know how and why to use specific technologies for specific projects simply because they are taking an online course. Digital literacy becomes part of our job when we teach literacy courses online. We cover digital literacy pedagogy in our other chapters.

Making sure that courses themselves are also accessible means that we use well-known methods, like captioning videos and alt text for images (which we cover in this text), but also making sure that activities and content are accessible linguistically, culturally, and experientially (Womack, 2017, p. 498). Because online courses become an archive of content (produced both by the instructor and the students), ensuring that courses are accessible in these ways is especially important. A useful framework for understanding access and accessibility beyond and inclusive of physical disabilities is Universal Design for Learning (UDL). UDL is a scholarly framework designed to support helping people learn. While this framework isn't intended only for online courses, it is particularly effective in providing theory and practice for accessible online courses (CAST, 2018).

Accessibility is an issue for all students (and teachers!). When thinking about the accessibility of a given text, we, as teachers, need to consider: hardware, software, connectivity, modality/media, as well as process knowledge. It is critical that we know the base accessibility standards, and hopefully a few adaptations, before assigning texts so that we can warn students what they'll need to be successful. As discussed in the Time and Social Justice section, considering time and student intersectionality are also important in making a course accessible. It's not *just* about the content and the technology.

We do want to acknowledge that making the "perfectly accessible" course is impossible. You can't possibly know and understand all of your individual students' needs (especially across the five areas below), and you will make choices in text and assignment design that make some of these easier or more difficult. Instead of thinking of accessibility as a checklist that you go through before classroom launch, think of it as a continuous set of considerations that you are always working toward improving. One term, you might explicitly work on making all of your digital documents accessible with alt tags and formatted headers. Another term, a student might prompt you to work with smaller screen restrictions. Your course will never be "accessible"; instead, it will always be "more accessible." We see the following sections as reference points that you'll be able to return to in order to continue making one small change at a time (Darby & Lang, 2019).

Accessibility Considerations

Hardware

This may, at first, seem like a simple consideration: My students have computers, so they can access the text. However, there are multiple elements of a text that can make accessibility more complex. Is this a long alphabetic text? Is it displayed in a responsive manner that can adapt to different-sized screens? Is this a high-resolution image? Do the monitor and graphics card have enough power to show it? Is it a complex image that needs to be viewed in its entirety? If so, what if most of your students are working from tablets, small laptops, or smartphones? For example, the device and hardware accessories available to a student (e.g., touchpad, mouse, roller ball) can impact the type of manipulations they might make in photo and image editing applications.

Hardware is not only about limitations. We are seeing some amazing advancements in XR (extended reality; e.g., augmented reality, AR; virtual reality, VR). Google Cardboard was (and the Google Cardboard App still is) an affordable way to have students access VR, assuming the students have access to a smartphone. The key point is to carefully assess the hardware requirements needed to access the texts you want students to engage with. If you haven't considered this before, you might start by going through your activities and listing out all the hardware students need to complete them as a way to begin accessing the accessibility of your requirements.

Software

We are often aware of the software programs that our institutions have access to. Not every school has Google accounts and not every school has Office 365. Making sure that students have access to the programs we want them to use and ensuring that the programs we use are accessible are critical elements.

Different types of texts require different applications for engagement. All PDF readers do not have the same built-in functions. Not all video players provide the ability to pause, rewind, slow down, and speed up the video. Many websites and web-based applications do not play well on all browsers. And don't forget that once you have a student accessing a text, you usually want them to somehow engage with it. Does the reader/viewer allow for annotation? Copying and remixing? Editing? (More on this in Chapters 5 and 6.)

Once you've designed your course or unit, carefully think about the software students will need in order to access the assigned texts and complete the work you will require. Instead of assuming students have this software, list software needs in the same way you list text(book) requirements. In our syllabi, we have changed the section formerly called "required (text)books" to "required materials." One small way to make sure software is accessible to students, and is a nice, next step to the hardware section, is to take the list you created and put it in a survey (like Learning Activity 2.1) that asks students if they know how to gain access to the programs and if their machines are able to access them.

Connectivity

We know, in this world of the ether and cloud, it seems weird to talk about physical connectivity, but physical connectivity is a reality. Internet connectivity is through wires and towers and satellites and devices; a missing link breaks down digital connectivity. A student may have the hardware and software to access and engage with the text, but if they don't have the connectivity, they are unable to access the course materials. If those physical objects are not accessible to the student to receive through the ether and the cloud, the text might as well not exist.

Students might also overestimate the quality of their connectivity. For example, students might report having consistent access to the internet, but it's through their mobile carrier. This might mean they're using a phone as a hotspot, or it might mean they're using their phone as their device. This is one of the reasons we ask the questions outlined in Learning Activity 2.1. If a student does lose their connectivity, we can be creative. Texts can still be conveyed through media such as CDs, DVDs, and thumb drives (be sure students have devices that can read what you plan to use), and some static alphabetic and image texts can be mailed. If you know your students have limited access (maybe they're going to the library or can only access when they have public Wi-Fi), you can carefully design and package materials so that they can easily download the texts and then work with them while offline. A small first step is to select large texts and videos and make them downloadable because they take the most bandwidth.

Process Knowledge

It's one thing to have the hardware, software, and media you need to access the text; it's another to know how to use these things. How many people had to be shown multiple times how to do a hanging indent in Word before they remembered how to do it themselves? If you are requiring your students to use specific software, like advanced features in Word or the graphics program

Canva, make sure you build in scaffolded "learn the technology" activities. These activities should focus on learning to use the technology in the ways that students need to use them for your intents and purposes of the course.

Process knowledge goes beyond the "how-to" of using a specific piece of software. Do students know common hardware and software issues, troubleshooting methods, or places they are likely to find help? For some, it's not necessarily common knowledge that some applications work better in one web browser than another. If you know your LMS works better in a particular browser (and most do!), tell your students. As another example, "Did you turn it off and on again?" is a frequent tech troubleshooting question for both hardware and software—do your students know to try that as a method to fix problems? We also can't assume students know that their browser keeps a cache of files and runs more smoothly (and sometimes fixes problems) if it is occasionally cleared. Students may not know that their digital textbook has an audio player or that the YouTube video player can be sped up or slowed down. The first time you assign something in a particular application, show students how to use the interface.

Universal Design for Learning and Multimodality

Universal Design for Learning is about providing alternative pathways and access to content, learning, and assessment. At minimum, if you are requiring your students to read a specific text, make sure they have access to an audio version of the text as well. If there are visual components to a text, then there should be alt text available for screen readers to access. A video or audio file should have a transcript. Making texts accessible is more than just providing the text through an alternative media like adding captions, headers, and alt text tags. In the same way that there are already a number of books to support teaching any class online, there are a number of web resources to help make media more accessible; we are not repeating that material here. Instead, we suggest you start by referencing CAST's website of UDL Guidelines. We want you to think of these adaptations for accessibility more expansively. It's not just about adapting the text; it's about providing a variety of access points to the text so that individuals, no matter the hardware or software they use to access the text, have an equitable experience. What you'll find, however, is that multiple access points also lead to better learning. As we mentioned earlier, this conversion of your course materials is what you ideally commit to changing over time.

Medium/Media/Modality

- **Medium:** the elements of art (e.g., a multimedia painting usually has pieces of other things in it).
- **Media:** the plural elements of digital art.
- **Modes:** reference the different sensory inputs—for example, receiving input through vision, hearing, taste, and touch (Mayer, 2021). And to make this more confusing, different media are engaged through different modes.

Providing a text through an alternate media is an adaptation, and that adaptation provides all of your students a new opportunity for accessing and understanding the content. Even if the point is to be teaching a specific version of the text (e.g., teaching the book, not the film version of a given text), comparisons and contrasts between the audio performance or the film adaptation of the text all contribute to a deeper understanding of the alphabetic text. Previously, we would have primarily used *modality* to reference different types of media (specifically, *modality* instead of *medium*), but since 2020, modality has come to mean the way that courses are delivered due to the pandemic (synchronous, asynchronous, in-person, hybrid, etc.). In this book, we use *medium* and *media*; independent of what we or you use, the point is to make sure your media is accessible.

In addition to being part of the technology scaffolding, prompting to find help needs to be built in. Part of being digitally literate is knowing when and how to find help. This is the case for both you and your students. If you and your students are going to predominantly teach and learn in digital environments, then you should start building a network of people and places (on campus and on the web) that can provide just-in-time support. You'll also want to ask students to go find resources for help as part of their work when producing with technologies.

Transitioning Ideas

This first part of the book establishes the foundations and principles of teaching online literacy courses. We don't continue pulling in scholarship, as the rest of the book focuses on the practical applications of what we've covered here. As you move through the different pieces of Parts 2 and 3, regardless of the order in which you explore them, it might be of value to occasionally return to Part 1 to reground yourself. At the beginning of each chapter, we tie our principles to the overarching ideas of that particular chapter, but this chapter serves as a good reminder of why those principles are so critical to what we do. As we look ahead to Chapter 4, remembering these principles as you help students establish their organizational methods will be critical to student success.

Websites and Applications

Calendly: https://calendly.com
Canva: https://www.canva.com/
D2L: https://d2l.com
Google Appointments: https://support.google.com/calendar/answer/190998
Google Cardboard VR: https://vr.google.com/cardboard/
Google Chats: https://chat.google.com
Microsoft Office 365: https://www.office.com/
Zoom: https://zoom.us

II

Teaching How to Find and Engage with Texts

Part 2 focuses on where and how instructors and students find, manage, read or view, analyze, and synthesize digital texts. For our purposes, "reading of texts" includes engagement prior to the annotating and note-taking activities. Dividing up reading engagement into discrete stages helps students pause and consider what they are reading and why they are reading. The point of the type of activities we're providing is not to hold students accountable for what went wrong; instead, the point is to allow them to reflect on what they learned from the experience and how they might do something differently the next time.

In this book, we refer to traditional written texts, like books, as "alphabetic texts." You may ask why we use the term alphabetic text instead of writing. As always, terminology quickly gets slippery. While we could say that everyone reads and writes all types of texts—alphabetic, images, audio, video, art, etc.—some feel more comfortable with terms like viewing, listening, composing, or producing. And although "consuming" texts also works for us and is well defended as an appropriate term by Schmidt and Kruger-Ross (2022), "consumption," as a term, carries negative cultural baggage. Since we want students to do more than just read or view or consume, we like using the term "engage." In short, deciding what terms to use with your students provides you with an opportunity to discuss language and word choice and the history associated with any given word or phrase. In this case, when we use "alphabetic text," we are referring to texts that are primarily made up of the written word. Obviously, traditional print texts usually fall into this category; however, again, you can quickly see the blurry boundaries when you start comparing things like children's picture books, coffee table books, and websites. Depending on the particular text in one of those genres, are they primarily alphabetic or visual texts? Similarly, although we are more likely to use "composing" or "producing" when talking about students working in media other than the written word, we also acknowledge the use of the term "writing" when discussing how a student weaves together images or sounds in a multimodal text.

Preparing to Find and Manage Digital Materials

4

Preparing to find and manage materials digitally gets its own chapter. Without an understanding of the ethics and legalities of finding texts and a solid organization method, you and your students might be in for a rough ride. Digital work makes it easy to find texts but also to inadvertently make unethical and potentially illegal mistakes. Digital work also makes it easy to misplace work you've found and already engaged with.

> ***Preparing Teachers and Students***
>
> The majority of the activities in Chapters 4 and 5 are just as relevant for teachers as for students. We safely assume that all teachers search for and use digital materials in their classes. Taking the time to carefully prepare search and management strategies will benefit you as a teacher as much as it will benefit your students. Instead of having separate chapters that would feel redundant, we frame most of the content in Chapter 4 toward assigning activities to your students. We hope you can easily reframe these activities to help with your own digital teaching activities. In Chapter 5, we more intentionally divide between search strategies for teachers and those for students.

While discussing legalities and management of finding texts in this chapter, we explicitly demonstrate the importance of our guiding principles for this book (as expressed in Chapter 3). The legalities associated with finding and using texts, especially copyright usages, are critical to understanding how texts circulate in both the learning environment of a class as well as in the larger social whole of a given discourse community. Further, the legalities get students thinking about access from different perspectives. After discussing potential legal issues, we move on to a section about managing digital texts. We emphasize managing before collecting because having a system in place before you search is critical to staying organized in the messy process that is research and writing. Strategies for finding and managing texts provide you with methods to help students understand what they do and do not have access to, how to manage their time, and how to prepare to share with one another.

Legalities for You and Your Students

Before finding texts, we want to make sure you and your students are aware of various legal issues surrounding the use of digital texts. On that "awareness" note, we are not lawyers; what we offer here is a collection of laws as we know them and apply them. Unless otherwise noted, most of the information below applies to any text, physical or digital. This is not the end-all-be-all of legalities in copyright law, but it should get you started. Many institutions and districts have lawyers or librarians who can explain in more detail if you have questions or concerns, and we recommend reaching out to your local resources.

Accessibility

When we discussed accessibility in Chapter 2, we emphasized the ethical importance of making your instructional materials accessible. In this chapter, especially if you are thinking about how to find and assign digital resources to your students, we want to remind you of the legal aspect of accessibility. If you teach in the public sector or if your private institution uses public funding (e.g., private institutions in higher education where students have access to and use federal financial aid), you are most likely required to abide by the Americans with Disabilities Act (ADA) and the Rehabilitation Act of 1973, Section 504. For teachers, this means students should not be denied access to instructional materials (and assessment practices) because of disability. Please revisit the section on Universal Design for Learning in Chapter 3 for a brief description about making your course, including the materials you share with students, accessible (for more details, visit CAST's website of UDL Guidelines).

Ethics in Finding and Collecting Texts and Materials

Copying versus Embedding

Ultimately, copyright is based upon making a new copy and distributing it. Therefore, if you download Martin Luther King Jr.'s *Letter from Birmingham Jail*, you have made a new copy that now resides on your computer. If you upload

>

it to your digital learning environment, you have now made another copy that resides there. And when each student downloads it to their computer to read, that many more copies are now floating around. Since MLK's "Letter" is a copyrighted text, you might want to link to the text you found originally instead of making a new copy.

Similarly, if you find an image of a painting on a museum's website and then download or take a screenshot of the image, you are making a new copy. However, if you grab the URL of where the image resides and embed the image in your course website, you would not be making a new copy. Embedding an image (or a video from YouTube or Vimeo) is like a visual link to the original digital text. Imagine that the space where you put the video (like your LMS) has a hole cut in it that sees through to the original posting of the image on the museum's website.

Embedding a text means you leave the original digital copy of the text where you found it and use computer code to cut the equivalent of a window in your web-based document that opens to the original and lets the visitors of your text see the media. In terms of copyright, when you have embedded something, you have not made a new copy; however, since you have not made a new copy, if the embedded text is moved or removed, your visual link will break.

Copyright

Copyright exists to protect intellectual property. This section isn't about the ethics of how large corporations, like Disney and others, have radically impacted copyright laws and policies. Instead, we just want you to be aware of copyright laws and fair-use policies. While not particular to digital spaces, digital spaces make it much easier to break copyright laws. The U.S. Copyright Act (2021) is federal legislation that prevents the copying and distribution of protected texts. Especially because of changing technologies, copyright now covers a variety of texts, including architectural design, software, visual arts, movies, and music.

Copying and distributing protected texts without permission can result in legal action. Illegal copying and distributing of protected works can include actions like:

- copying pages of a book and handing them out;
- showing films in class (or posting them to a learning management system); and

- using images in presentations.

All of these potentially break copyright if the text is not licensed in a way that allows for that kind of sharing or if you do not have permission from the author or other copyright holder. Therefore, if you are looking for materials for students to read, view, or listen to as part of your course, you'll want to make sure that they are one of the following:

- in the public domain (out of copyright);
- appropriately licensed (either you or your school purchased them to be used with students or they have other licensing such as Creative Commons discussed below);
- allowed to be used because the author or copyright holder has granted permission; or
- used within the scope of the guidelines for Fair Use or the TEACH Act.

Fair Use

When using texts in educational settings, our usage often falls under fair use. Fair use is a framework that allows for the use of copyrighted materials without permission within specific contexts. Section 107 of the Copyright Act (2021) provides the four following factors to assess whether or not the use of the text falls within fair use:

- "Purpose and character of the use, including whether the use is of a commercial nature or is for nonprofit educational purposes;
- Nature of the copyrighted work;
- Amount and substantiality of the portion used in relation to the copyrighted work as a whole; and
- Effect of the use upon the potential market for or value of the copyrighted work."

For example, if you want to teach about gender roles, you might show clips from various Disney movies. As long as you are teaching in a nonprofit setting, only show pieces from the films, and appropriately cite the sources from which the clips originated, then your use of the clips falls within fair use. In this case, since you did not show the entire film, it does not hurt the potential value of the film (students may still decide to go purchase the film to watch it in its entirety).

Some might argue that showing any entire film within class falls under fair use; we again want to remind you that we are not lawyers and are providing a more conservative interpretation of fair use because it is an ethical concern. When we teach students about plagiarism, being consistent and modeling appropriate behavior is important.

Based on our conservative (and safer) interpretation, if you simply show a copyrighted film to keep students "busy" during a class period, that does *not* fall under fair use. Similarly, if an instructor uses a static screenshot from a film at the beginning of a slide presentation in a way that is not directly connected to the topic under instruction or the theme of the presentation, that too does not fall within fair-use guidelines. When we work with faculty finding and using copyrighted material, we usually emphasize:

- **Purpose and character of use**: Are you able to clearly articulate how and why the text supports the lesson or topic being covered?
- **Effect upon the value**: Do you share the entire work in such a way that someone would not purchase or access it otherwise? Do you restrict the sharing of the work to just students in the class, or is the work made publicly available?

Therefore, if the first slide of a presentation about gender roles is a picture of a Disney princess, and you prompt students to do a freewrite about that image prior to the lesson, the use of the image should easily fall within fair-use guidelines.

The TEACH Act

In 2002, Congress enacted the "Technology, Education and Copyright Harmonization Act," commonly known as the "TEACH Act." It is a full revision of Section 110(2) of the U.S. Copyright Act, focused on using copyrighted materials for distance learning. Among other things, the TEACH Act asks instructors to carefully focus on when, where, and how students are accessing copyrighted materials. First, it prompts us to think about whether or not we must make a new copy of the text. In other words, if the copyrighted text is legally posted in a public website, you should link to that text instead of making a new copy to post within the LMS. Second, if a copyrighted text is posted within the digital classroom for educational purposes, the TEACH Act calls on us to make sure that:

1. only students enrolled in the class are allowed to access the text, and
2. the text is taken back down (made inaccessible) once the lesson or course is complete.

With its focus on digital education, the TEACH Act prompts us to think carefully about the digital distribution of copyrighted material.

While not part of the TEACH Act, asking students to find and use texts for their own work also needs to account for copyright and fair use. Just because a student is producing a video for class does not mean they are using the copyrighted text for educational purposes. Although using copyrighted material to help *teach* something is clearly protected under fair use, whether those protections extend to students using materials they find to *learn* something is not 100 percent clear. Therefore, we highly emphasize that you should require students to use materials that are legally licensed for remixing, like those in the public domain or with Creative Commons licensing (discussed in the next section). As an instructor, prompt students to think about where and how they will distribute their final work and whether or not it includes copyrighted materials. If you plan to have students produce texts that might use copyrighted images, audio, video, or other texts, you might want to provide an activity that teaches them about copyright and fair use. This activity, in an online course, should include some getting started texts and videos like our favorites: Brigham Young University's (2017) *It's a Wonderful Law* and Eric Faden's *A Fair(y) Use Tale*. Then, "learn the concept" activities are a good place to ask students to go find some resources. For example, you might ask students to search the web for resources on public domain, copyright, and fair use and then share their findings and read each other's resources. This becomes a sort of jigsaw activity that helps students to search broadly but also to see consistent themes throughout the information. While deciding what digital materials to use, it will be critical to make sure students are aware that if they're going to claim fair use because they're making an educational project, they won't be able to use the project with copyrighted material in a public e-portfolio or for any other purpose than the course.

Creative Commons

Creative Commons is a nonprofit copyright licensing organization that provides a variety of licenses to original work (varying from "you can't use this" to "feel free!"). The Creative Commons website also provides a search engine to help find multimedia artifacts that are licensed for reuse.

Many assume that for a text to be protected under copyright, creators must apply for copyright protection when, in fact, unless licensed otherwise, both published and unpublished works are covered by copyright upon production. As such, if people want to license their work for reuse, they have to explicitly license it in another way than the default of copyright. Creative Commons licensing provides creators with the ability to license their work in different ways.

Please note that just because a resource is licensed for reuse doesn't necessarily mean it is licensed to be remixed or edited into a new text. Be sure to pay close attention to the licensing before you decide whether you or your students are:

1. using the text as is;
2. adding the resource to your own text without changing it (remixing with other texts, which means you are developing a new text); or
3. editing it further (again, this means you are developing a new text).

If you are going to have students search and use Creative Commons licensed materials, you might want to have them read and learn about Creative Commons first—for instance, add a Creative Commons layer to the copyright activity suggested above.

Attribution

Whether you or your students are using something that is copyrighted or Creative Commons licensed and whether you or they uploaded or embedded it, no matter what, you or they *must* provide adequate attribution. Attribution is important for two reasons:

1. to give credit where credit is due and
2. to provide a trail back to where you originally found the media.

When including attribution or citations in different types of media, you do not necessarily need to be thinking in terms of scholarly citation style like MLA and APA. Instead, make sure you and your students cite in such a way that:

- distinguishes the work that isn't yours;
- provides a path back to where you found the original text; and
- does not disrupt the flow of your own text.

For example, many blog authors use hyperlinks to mark and link back to texts they are discussing or citing. Video producers, however, like scholarly authors, usually leave their citations for the end of the text or in the roll of credits.

> ***Attributing AI-Generated Materials***
>
> Throughout this book, we provide some suggestions for how you might prompt students to incorporate generative AI technologies as part of their research, reading, and production processes. If you decide to incorporate such activities into your classes, you'll want to explicitly discuss where and how students will document and attribute when, where, and how they used AI technologies. For ideas to help students keep track of their process, see the Reflective Research Journals section later in this chapter.

Notice that embedded YouTube videos include a link back to the page where the video is posted on YouTube—the citation is built into the embedding code. However, if you use a URL to embed an image into your website such that you are not making another copy, you are probably not including enough attribution materials and need to add something else that references an author, title, and location. Citing other media within your digital media text is rarely easy; however, it is important that you and your students do so. You might ask students to analyze examples of the types of texts they are using or producing to see how the examples give attribution to other resources (for example, Learning Activity 8.1 in Chapter 8).

Ethics in Collecting Personal Experiences and Data

If students are writing about their own experiences, they may feel like they do not necessarily need to worry about any ethical considerations. We would like to remind you, and through you your students, that privacy is always a consideration. These are your students' memories; so, you and they should feel fine sharing them, correct? But what if they are talking about previous experiences that include information about what *other* people did or said? Do they have the right to share those details? And, if we acknowledge that memories are not perfect, it could be even worse if they share a misremembered detail about someone that casts that individual in a negative light. The ethics associated with collecting, analyzing, and sharing memoires is deeply connected to the purpose for which and the audience with whom the student shares the final presentation. In *Decolonizing Methodologies: Research and Indigenous Peoples*, Linda Tuhiwai Smith (2012) provides questions for researchers to think about regarding the point, purpose, and potential impact of their research.

- Who defined the research problem?
- For whom is this study worthy and relevant? Who says so?
- What knowledge will the community gain from this study?
- What knowledge will the researcher gain from this study?
- What are some likely positive outcomes from this study?
- What are some possible negative outcomes?
- How can the negative outcomes be eliminated?
- To whom is the researcher accountable?
- What processes are in place to support the research, the researched, and the researcher? (175–76).

When asking students to conduct research, even collecting details from their own memories, you might ask students to reflect upon similar questions.

Primarily, we want to remind you that people have a right to privacy. If you ask students to collect data about or data generated by other people, you generally need the permission of those people. If you ask students to make observations in public places, they might not need to get permission from the people present during the observation. Please remember, however, that even when in public places, many people assume that others are not paying attention. For example, although individuals may post replies to a digital forum that is publicly available to any reader, they generally assume only those interested in the topic and engaged in the forum are the ones reading. If students are remembering events or people, they are potentially sharing private details about those places or individuals. Similarly, if they are producing texts that will be shared with you, their classmates, and potentially others outside of the class, students need to be prepared for people to comment upon their own private actions and reactions.

If your students interview and conduct surveys, they should always get permission or consent of the person providing the data. If you are a college instructor, please check with your Human Subjects Review team or Institutional Research office before asking students to collect primary data (especially interviews or surveys).

Once students are producing multimedia texts that represent their memories, they might also need to think about what objects are within the pictures or videos they share or what music they are using to express themselves. Content within pictures, videos, and soundtracks may be copyrighted materials. If you plan to prompt students to develop multimedia texts, you still might want them to complete something like Learning Activity 5.3: Preparing to Search for Digital

Images so that they are evaluating texts for content, format, licensing, and ethical or privacy considerations.

Managing Digital Texts

We would argue many people miss a critical step between finding and using digital texts: organizing and managing. In other words, once they have found the text, what do they do with it until they are ready to use it in their research or multimedia project? When working in digital spaces, a management plan is critical to track what you have, where it is, and what you still need. Starting without a management plan and organization method can lead to losing materials (we're guilty of having downloaded the same article multiple times because we can't remember what we called it and where we put it) and being unable to easily connect ideas. Fortunately, with the right tools (or combination of tools), digital management can make all the difference.

The key is making the plan at the start, and that goes for both you and your students. Selecting where students are going to do the reflecting, the storing, and the note-taking is important, but understanding how those pieces will point back to each other is the golden ticket. In the following section, you'll find key considerations to weigh before jumping in to collect texts; in Chapter 6 are considerations for managing annotations (notes on the text), and Chapter 7 has considerations for managing notes that are external to the text. Be sure to build your plan for students with consideration for how these stages work together or have your students work through their own plans with that in mind.

Most of us have our notes, plans, ideas, and lives in more than one digital location. Students might be given or might find texts to be bookmarked or downloaded, and a combination of these two methods of collection is most likely. This necessitates a plan for tracking and organizing the process and the texts. You might have students do this in a program like Notion, Trello, PowerNotes, or even something as simple as a word-processing document listing where they're keeping specific types of texts. Each method has affordances and constraints, but, as many learned during the pandemic, clearly articulating what goes where and how to find what you need are key elements. We suggest establishing this at the start so your students don't have folders called "stuff for class" or untitled PDFs on their computer that they can't find later. Depending on the level of your students, you might articulate exactly how and where you want things organized or you might simply ask students to create their own plan, share it with you, and stick to it.

A good organization method needs a system for where to keep specific types of texts, a naming system that spans across all of those spaces, and a way to keep track of what they've done. The more common management methods for texts (either born digital or made digital) are bookmarking, source-tracking, and downloading. Each of these methods has a section later in this chapter. Naming conventions might include the student's last name, the title of the course, the semester/year, the title of the text being used, and even where it's going to be used (like in project 1 or as background music). You'll also want to assign or create the space for students to keep track of their progress and text locations. These pieces should be decided from the start in order to keep you and your students organized. In this section, many of our suggestions are for students but can easily be adapted for your own purposes. You might already have your own practice, but we suggest that everyone have space to do the following:

- reflect on progress and process; and
- track what's being collected in ways that are useful for future retrieval.

If these two spaces are different, you'll want to make sure that there is a way to connect them through linking, a folder, or whatever way makes sense to you and your students.

Reflective Research Journals

Part of a good organization method goes beyond collecting and tracking the sources. Using well-designed digital journaling environments will help students continue a reflective practice in order to prepare for future projects. Because reading and researching is a multimodal endeavor, we suggest that instructors assign note-taking in digital spaces. Specifically, consider introducing students to digital spaces that have the affordances of searching and sorting. The goal of these notes is to provide a reflective space to help students track progress, process, and the locations of the texts they're collecting. Some robust digital note-taking environments might include:

- **Blogs**: Blogs are probably the easiest to start because they are by default set up as journaling environments. Have students produce a single entry for each source or type of data. Prompt students to use the tagging (e.g., labels) feature by tagging entries with keywords from the notes. Students can then use the tags/labels to sort through the entries.

- **Spreadsheets and Databases**: By developing their own databases or spreadsheets, students can make their own types of categories with which to sort through sources. If they are taking short snippets of notes, they might keep the notes in a spreadsheet. If they have longer notes, consider posting them in a Google Doc and then using the spreadsheet to code, sort, and link to the longer notes.
- **Robust Note-Taking Applications**: Teachers and students are not the only ones who need robust note-taking applications. Many technology companies have produced note-taking applications that provide the ability to easily tag, search, and sort notes. Most of them also allow users to share notes and/or notebooks with others (including teachers who might be skimming/grading student work).

Technology Toolbox: Robust Note-Taking Applications

- PowerNotes
- OneNote
- Evernote
- Scrivener
- Notion
- Trello

And if these are all too complex—and we admit, sometimes they *are,* for our purposes—you might revert to notes in a single document. If you have students taking reading notes in a single digital document, instruct them to use headings and heading formatting so they can automatically generate a detailed table of contents (at the top of the document or a document outline in the left-hand margin of the document). This will allow you and them to navigate around these notes with ease. As with all technologies in online literacy classes, you'll want to be sure to select a technology that fits your needs; we imagine programs like PowerNotes, Evernote, OneNote, and Scrivener work here due to their affordances. When assigning journals, you might create a template for students to use with reflective questions that shift depending on where the group is in the project (see Learning Activity 4.1).

Learning Activity 4.1: Research Journal

<h1>Intro Header

<h2>Prepare

(*Instructor insert: Select a technology that you've already used in the course. You might have students use a word-processing document and ensure new journal titles and dates use headings so that students can easily generate a table of contents, or encourage students to use a blog that allows for the easy start and organization of new posts. Ideally, you should only need the student to publish or share the journal document with you once, and you will see all their resulting posts thereafter.)

<h2>Write/Add

1. To get in the habit of documenting your research, post an entry each time you work on your research project.
2. For each new research journal entry, start a title at the top of the page with the date and a descriptive title for the entry (e.g., collecting data, analyzing data, reflecting on themes, etc.). For example: "7/27/22: Reading Sources, Interesting Themes." When you start a new entry, begin at the top of the page (which will push the older entries down).
3. In your entries, you might want to answer the following types of questions:
    - What did you search for or otherwise do during the session?
    - What did you find?
    - Where did you put it?
    - What do you still need to find?
    - What will you do next time?

<h2>Submission

When you submit your project, be prepared to submit your research journal to the assignment folder as well.

<h2>Rubric/Grading Criteria

There are a variety of ways you might design and implement a rubric for a journal assignment. In the initial prompt, you can list the total number of entries required and then outline the elements required in each entry. For example: "You will submit at least five posts over the life of the project (4 points each × 5 posts = 20 points). Each post will include:

- date (1 point each);
- descriptive title (1 point each);
- description of completed work (1 point each); and
- reflection or connection about the work (1 point each).

Or you might provide specific reminders of journal entries at specific points during the course or project. If you assign each post individually, you can fine-tune the entry requirements based on the work students are currently doing with the project. In order to be cognizant of students' time and energy, we suggest you provide opportunities for as much credit as possible and stick to observable tasks.

Organization Methods

This section provides a few different options for keeping track of texts. Some, like spreadsheets, will provide students space to both track and reflect because of the ability to create multiple sheets in a workbook. Others, like bookmarking, will need to be used in conjunction with a separate reflective space if the tool doesn't afford space for additional text. Regardless, these two pieces—reflective space and tracking space—should be established at the beginning.

Bookmarking

Since we're talking about finding digital texts, in most cases, the texts can be bookmarked using a browser. There are two problems with having students use their personal browsers: 1) the bookmarks are only saved to their personal browser system (which requires exporting bookmarks in order to share them with either the instructor or other classmates), and 2) there is no space to leave brief notes about what is being saved. At a minimum, have students copy and paste URLs into shared word-processing documents or discussion board posts, or have them bookmark and export the URLs. Just keep in mind that exporting bookmarks will export a list of *all* of their bookmarks, so they'll want to organize them into folders to make the copy-and-paste process easier. However, asking students to bookmark what they find in resources like Hypothes.is or PowerNotes makes it easier for them to share the results as well as to leave brief notes about why and how they might use the resource. If the resource is going to be carefully read and analyzed later, already having it bookmarked in one of these note-taking applications at the "finding" stage will help.

One of the main benefits of starting with simply bookmarking is that the student has not yet made a copy of the text—they've only left a link or a trail to it. Note that once that text is actually downloaded, a copy has been made, and therefore you need to carefully consider copyright laws.

Source Trackers and Citation Generators

Multiple source-tracking programs also support note-taking and citation generation. Ensuring students understand the affordances and constraints of each tool before selecting one is important.

Technology Toolbox: Popular Source-Tracking and Citation-Generating Applications

- Zotero
- PowerNotes
- Mendeley
- EndNote
- RefWorks

If we're choosing for our students, we need to be transparent about our choices and why we picked the tool. If we're letting students choose, we need to guide students through the process of identifying the affordances and limitations of the tools they select. You might help students do this by assigning students to first:

- Identify their needs in a source tracker and citation generator, reviewing tools based on how well they fit their needs.
- Create a plan for tracking sources that includes steps utilizing the functions they felt would be most useful to them.

Since committing to a source tracker and citation generator can be a big decision (especially for students starting big research projects or longer-term careers as researchers), helping them understand the affordances and constraints associated with different functionalities will save them time and frustration both during the information/source-collecting process and later when finalizing their projects. Most of these applications have citation-generation abilities for multiple citation styles. Most also have at least one area in which a student can leave notes about the text. However, not all of these applications have the ability to easily collaborate on making and editing source lists, especially over time.

For example, we especially like how Zotero allows users to attach tags (e.g., codes, key terms) to *both* the overall source references as well as the individual notes associated with the source. Therefore, if in one class a student uses a source for a paper, they can take notes on the source within Zotero. If that student uses the same source for another paper two terms later, they can start a separate note, acknowledging that what they need from the source is likely to be slightly different. The two different notes might have different tags/codes/key terms that are more aligned with the different purposes and projects. The functionality to provide both source and note-specific tags allows the user to sort through the resulting database of sources and notes in a more complex and nuanced manner. Whereas this might not be as useful or relevant to a student just using a source manager for a single semester, this functionality would be critical to a student starting a research topic and/or project that would span multiple classes and terms. By understanding what they need from their source tracker and citation generator, students will make better decisions when they select which application to use.

Assigning source managers can be difficult when it comes to assessment. Most of the applications have the ability to create annotated bibliography-style notes for all the sources in the application or all the sources associated with a project. Increasingly, many of them allow the user to either share or collaborate on lists—which means a student can share their list with an instructor. At a minimum, instructors can ask students to periodically take and share screenshots of their work within a source manager.

Since these applications are more complex to learn (they're basically databases!), carefully consider your student population and the project before assigning a specific source-tracker or citation-manager application. Make sure the project and the students' potential long-term use of the application are worth the time and cognitive effort to learn and use.

Instead of source trackers or citation managers, students can simply use a spreadsheet to track sources. Although the spreadsheet will not be able to generate citations in different formats, it can still allow students to track sources and start taking notes.

Learning Activity 4.2: Preparing to Track Sources

<h1>Intro Header

<h2>Prepare

Create a table in Word, Excel, or Google Docs or Sheets. Title your document: <LastName>-TrackingSources-Course-SemesterYear.

In your table, include at least five columns and seven rows. In the five columns across the top, write:

- Title of source (or author and year of publication)
- Full bibliographic citation
- Summary
- How/why does this source help answer the research question?
- How/why is this source authoritative and/or credible?
- **(*Instructor insert: Insert other categories or framework elements students should use to analyze the sources or texts they're reading; if you add elements, add to the number of columns.)**

(*Instructor suggestion: You may want to make a template document or spreadsheet that students can use to copy and start their own documents. See the "Learning Activity 4.2" tab in Secondary Research Note-Taking Spreadsheet linked example.)

1	**Focused Topic/Research Question:**					
2	**Title of Source (or Author & Year of Publication)**	**Full Bibliographic Citation**	**Summary**	**How/why does this sources help answer the research question?**	**How/why is this source authoritative and/or credible?**	**Other Notes**
3						
4						
5						
6						
7						
8						
9						

FIGURE 4.1. Example of Note-Taking Spreadsheet

>

QR 4.1. *Secondary Research Note-Taking Spreadsheet*
Provide students with a spreadsheet in which they can take organized notes: https://tlo.pub/spreadsheet

<h2>Write/Add

1. At the top of the document, write your focused research topic, question, or thesis.
2. Fill in a row for every source you have collected and read.
3. Make sure you complete a row of information for at least 6 sources.

<h2>Submit and Reflect

Upload the completed document to the assignment area. In the comment area, briefly reflect upon your research thus far:

1. What have you learned about your topic thus far?
2. What do you still want or need to learn more about?

<h2>Rubric/Grading Criteria

(*Instructor suggestion: This is just a process step in which you scan to see if students have completed the work—basically to confirm they have a completed table for the minimum number of sources you assign. If you must closely check their note-taking, try focusing on only one column [inform them you'll be focusing on the third column of every student submission]. The point of this activity is to make sure students are not trying to do all the secondary research and reading the night before a formal project is due. Consider assigning this type of assignment two or three times before a major project is due, requiring an increasing number of entries each time.)

You need to separate the "Preparing to Track Sources" activity from an actual reading and tracking-sources activity. You should emphasize setup, including specifics for document title as well as row and column titles. The rubric for filling out the spreadsheet should require completing a row for the minimum number of sources as well as a reflection; as in Learning Activity 4.2, your reflection might be broken down into multiple sections as well. The transparency of focusing on the tasks in assessment allows both student choices as well as a move toward unbiased assessment.

Downloading and Organizing

Despite the plethora of cloud-based applications that help us organize and manage texts, some texts we find digitally might still need to be downloaded (or saved in a cloud repository), specifically if they're going to be used in a multimedia project.

> ***Technology Toolbox: Digital Repositories***
>
> - Google Drive
> - Dropbox
> - OneDrive
> - Box
> - Notion

Downloading creates a new copy. (Again, this is why we highly suggest finding and using media that is licensed for reuse.) Downloading media files has become increasingly easier, especially those that are licensed for reuse. As such, if a text is difficult to find and download, it might be because the digital protections are set to guard it at the copyright level.

Once digital texts are downloaded, managing them becomes messy. How do you title the files? Where do you store them? As with searching for digital texts, a little preparation goes a long way toward managing digital texts (see Learning Activity 4.3).

> ***Learning Activity 4.3: Preparing to Organize Digital Materials***
>
> **<h1>Intro Header**
>
> ***<h2>Read***
>
> **(*Instructor insert: links to resources about file-naming conventions)**
>
> ***<h2>Needs Identification***
>
> First, identify why you need and how you will use the digital materials.
>
> 1. Why do you need the digital materials?
> 2. How will you be using them for your future project?
> 3. What applications will you be using to access and use them? Do those applications require that the files be located in a specific location? If so, where? **(*Instructor note: If your students are downloading resources for producing a video, they are especially likely to need**
>
> >

to carefully store the files in such a way as to easily access them when working within the video editing application.)

4. Do the texts have easily identifiable authors? Titles? Year of production or distribution? How and why might that information be useful in the file title?

<h2>Plan

Based on the answers above, design a plan for where and how you will save your downloaded texts. Your plan should include:

- Location of where you will keep your digital artifacts.
    - Discussion of how and why this location works best for you, for this particular project, and for sharing with your instructor and the class.
        - For this project in this course, you may start your digital folder in one of the following locations: Box, Dropbox, Google Drive, or OneDrive.
        - **(*Instructor note: You may decide it is easier to just assign where everyone will keep the files in the same place or that they can choose two or three options.)**
- Naming convention for your files.
    - Discussion of how and why this naming convention works best for you, for this particular project, and for sharing with your instructor and the class.

<h2>Prepare

Start your project in a shared folder within the digital repository you selected. Be sure to title it according to your naming conventions and provide appropriate permissions so that the instructor and all your classmates can **(*Instructor insert: Describe in detail the appropriate settings)**.

<h2>Submission

In the LMS submission area, provide a link to your shared digital repository folder. Upload your plan document into the folder.

Transitioning Ideas

This chapter centers on finding, acquiring, and organizing texts. These are the first steps for both you and your students before using the texts for a variety of purposes. Breaking down these steps into manageable activities and asking students to reflect on the choices they make in collecting and organizing texts is vital to laying the foundation for students to read and process the information in the texts they're collecting. In the next chapter, we cover the actual collecting and management of texts.

Websites and Applications

Box: https://www.box.com/
CAST UDL Guidelines: https://udlguidelines.cast.org/
Creative Commons: https://creativecommons.org/
Dropbox: https://www.dropbox.com/
EndNote: https://endnote.com/
Evernote: https://evernote.com/
Google Docs: https://docs.google.com/
Google Drive: https://www.google.com/drive/
Mendeley: https://www.mendeley.com/
Notion: https://www.notion.so/
OneDrive: https://www.microsoft.com/en-us/microsoft-365/onedrive/online-cloud-storage
OneNote: https://www.onenote.com/
PowerNotes: https://powernotes.com/about
RefWorks: https://refworks.proquest.com/
Scrivener: https://www.literatureandlatte.com/scrivener/overview
Trello: https://trello.com/
Zotero: https://www.zotero.org/

5

Collecting and Managing Digital Materials

Now that you know about some of the legal issues surrounding sharing and using texts and are prepared to save and track them, we are finally at the "how-to" and "what to consider" stages of finding texts for your students and having them find texts on their own. We imagine both you and your students will likely need to find texts to read, edit, and remix for the course. In education, we have multiple reasons to "find" texts and information: We find them to read about and understand a topic; we find them to support arguments about a topic; and we find them to address complex problems. Whether you are finding texts for students or asking students to find them for themselves, the ease of finding texts on the internet is how and why the internet has greatly changed education.

Although literacy learning is often associated with reading and writing texts, we, and many librarians we have worked with over the years, argue that finding the appropriate texts to read, remix, and use is a critical aspect of literacy as well. And if you are teaching your courses through and in digital environments, you'll need to be cognizant of finding texts students can access or helping students find texts on their own. Discussing strategies for finding and managing texts also provides you with the opportunity to explicitly discuss text selection and access and time management as forms of social justice. This chapter is divided into two major sections: "Collecting for Students" and "Having Students Collect." Each scenario requires a different approach to ensure that we're following the guidelines of accessibility. We do not spend as much time explicitly sharing assignments on selecting and evaluating texts because we assume most literacy educators already have a number of example activities prompting evaluative work.

Using Generative AI to Find Texts

As generative AI applications become more entrenched as part of our researching, reading, and producing practices, students might want to

>

prompt AI apps to find appropriate texts for them. The way the prompt is worded will greatly impact the results, and if the prompt asks for something the AI app doesn't specifically have, it is likely to make up the results to fulfill the request. In other words, AI applications do not understand user qualifiers (i.e., "I'm not sure about ABC, but I think XYZ") and instead just provide what appears to be a definitive answer (i.e., "XYZ is the answer!"). It is critical that users of any given AI application know the archive or corpus from which the AI derives its models. Does the AI app have access to anything after a certain year? Does it have access to the databases that include scholarly, peer-reviewed articles and books? No matter what, they'll need to check the AI-referenced text to be certain first that it exists and that it's what they're looking for.

Collecting Texts and Materials for Students

If you're the one collecting texts and materials for your students, be sure that not only can students get ahold of the text but that they can view/read/etc. what you're providing. The following sections articulate what to look for as you're considering the accessibility of texts for your students.

Physical Texts

Of course, not everything is digital, even if you're working and teaching in a digital space! You might need to find and use texts that only exist in the real world. Even if you are referencing or sharing a physical text, we suggest that, if allowed, you might still want to digitally record the text for future reference and use. Some texts and materials that you want to include as part of your course only exist in real life. For example, bumper stickers on a car that contextualize each other to create meaning, real-life sounds that create a mood, and handwritten recipes or letters all live in the physical world and may not be digitized yet (or you might not like the versions that are already digitized). The easiest way to capture physical texts for a digital course environment is to somehow record the text (e.g., audio, image, or video). Before doing so, however, first make sure you are legally able to record and share that text. Then, we highly recommend that you make multiple recordings of the text so you can select the best one to use.

You may be very familiar with assigning students to read a physical copy of an alphabetic text. When teaching online, however, you'll want to make sure your students can obtain physical copies and that there are copies or versions available to students with disabilities (e.g., audio files and larger or adaptable fonts). When assigning alphabetic texts in digital environments, make sure students have the option to purchase or print a hard copy of the text. Audio and visual texts need alternative access options as well. For example, if you're assigning a specific movie to watch or an audio file to listen to that is not digital (for example, some college libraries have copies of films that they are not allowed to digitize), you'll want to be sure that students are able to get a copy from a library or streaming service; however, keep in mind that libraries may only have one copy. In this situation, it might help to also schedule a few screening times so that more than one student can view the film at the same time. Obviously, if most of your online students are not in the same general vicinity, scheduled screenings will be more difficult to manage. You'll need to find out (using something like the survey in Learning Activity 2.1) where students are and how they might access hard copies. Digitizing texts that are not currently available so that you can make them available for your students for a limited period of time might fall under the TEACH Act; talk to a school administrator, librarian, or legal expert before converting and sharing.

Digital Texts

One of the joys of teaching in the twenty-first century is the accessibility to vast numbers of texts that have been digitized so you and your students can easily find, see, and engage with them. Each day, more and more physical texts are made digitally available; for example, many libraries are slowly digitizing their own archive collections. (Catrina was very excited when *Garfield's Holiday Specials* DVD finally found its way to a digital library!)

Alphabetic

Digital alphabetic texts can be found in a variety of places. Some textbooks make epublications; the library (either your institution's or the local library) has ebooks and articles that are prepaid. In essence, the internet is an endless trove of alphabetic-based texts. When deciding what you want to assign, you also have to consider where you and your students are going to get it. Are you giving it to them, or are they finding it on their own? Is it accessible widely on the web? Is it behind a paywall (and does your school already have access to those resources)? Are you legally able to make a copy of the text, or do you have to link the students to the material? Especially if you and the students are able to make new copies of the text, you might need to decide what you will be asking students to do with the text. Will they simply be reading it? Will they be annotating and taking notes on it (Chapter 6)? Will they use it for synthesizing across multiple texts (Chapter 7)?

If the digital alphabetic text is something you are giving students to read, you'll want to make sure that it's accessible to those with disabilities (like those who need screen readers). Selecting the where and how the materials are made available is going to be just as important as deciding what to share. For example, if a PDF hasn't been converted to Optical Character Recognition (OCR), then a screen reader won't be able to read it to the student. Sometimes, even if the document *is* converted to OCR, the information at the bottom of each page that has nothing to do with the content (like page numbers or urls or access dates) are being read as well, which makes the text much less accessible to blind students. We recommend you reach out to your resources—your institution or district should have a disability specialist or center that can work with you on those documents. However, making sure you have enough time to be confident that all reading materials are inherently accessible is important. And, as we said in Chapter 3, *all* students benefit from accessible texts.

Images

Finding static images on the web is just as easy as finding alphabetic texts. The difference, however, is that locating the licensing option of the image is usually much more difficult. If you are searching for images to use for presentations or other class activities, we recommend you start your search with databases and search engines designed to easily sort images based on licenses. In fact, we encourage you to show students how to do this as well after you have determined the how and where of the particular image you want. In other words, show students Unsplash, the Creative Commons search engine, and Flickr, and demonstrate how to filter Google Image search results based on usage rights. You can also use sites like TinEye and Google Images to upload images and try to locate where they were originally distributed. Model the act of image searching during a lesson or video, where you have prepared in advance what you will search for and know what you'll find and how to get there as you walk students through it. Don't forget: when you are teaching through digital technologies, keep instructional videos like the one suggested above to a reasonable length and reduce the amount of accidental clicking in a video-conferencing session.

Audio and Video

Finding and using audio and video resources, especially those licensed for reuse, can be even more difficult. In these cases, you are not only looking for specific content, but you also need to pay close attention to the format in which it exists.

For example, your digital teaching environment may only be able to upload and show MP4 videos, so you'll need to make sure the video you find is in that format (or that it provides you with an embedding code instead).

Having Students Collect Texts and Materials

For students, collection might be finding texts and materials that already exist, or it might be generating those texts and materials for use in class. When students research and produce projects about other topics, they need to collect primary and secondary data as well as digital artifacts about said topics. While producing more personal projects like memoirs, students might use digital applications to help generate, collect, analyze, and synthesize personal data. When students write about themselves, they collect primary data based on their previous experiences and memories and, as outlined earlier in the chapter, still need to collect, store, and organize the artifacts they collect and generate.

Physical Texts

Just as you might want to use physical texts, your students may as well. This might be a step for a larger project about a personal experience or those physical texts might be what they observe or analyze for their projects. This kind of scaffolding requires having an idea of what students will do with it. For example, if you have students collecting or generating physical texts to help generate content for a personal project, like a literacy narrative, a "This I Believe" project, or an "I Search" project, you might already have activities in which you ask students to explore their memories and experiences. If you want students to share or use the physical texts they're collecting, like snippets of a handwritten recipe or a print photograph, they'll need to digitize them. As you send students off to collect these pieces, you'll want to have students identify the technology they'll use to digitize those texts and where to find help to do so.

> ***Hidden Privileges***
>
> Assuming that students can easily digitize artifacts they found at home is a dangerous assumption for an instructor. Let's walk through the steps to better understand how much access and previous experience can impact a student's process:
>
> >

1. The student must have ready access to a device that can digitally record pictures, video, or audio of the quality level required for the assignment. If the student or someone with whom they live does not have a device, they will have to spend extra time accessing a device.
2. The student must know how to:
    - use the software on the device to digitally capture the artifact;
    - locate the digital file on the device and confirm file type (and, if needed, convert to a required file type); and
    - transfer the digital file to where it is required to be for the course assignment.

Students who have less experience recording and transferring digital files will likely spend a lot more time simply *recording* materials. And if they struggle, their frustration is likely to negatively impact their work and learning as they continue with the project (Cavanagh, 2016).

What follows are types of materials we typically have students collecting in a personal project that are usually related to real-life experiences; therefore, we've categorized them as physical texts. For each type of material, we have suggestions for you and your students:

- **Photos and Material Objects**: We suggest keeping a copy of the image(s) or taking a picture of the object(s) and storing them within a digital notebook.
- **Spaces and Places**: Prompt students to go to specific spaces and places related to the topic they are hoping to remember. Again, since they might be working in digital spaces, consider reminding them to record themselves (via audio or video) as they move about the space and to talk about what they remember. At a minimum, require that they take pictures of the space or place and complete a written memory dump, keeping the pictures and writing together. You might want to suggest they move through the space in a systematic manner so they don't miss any details.
- **Recorded Texts**: A variety of texts may include lots of details about an individual: birth certificates, school transcripts, medical transcripts, pictures or videos of sporting or family events, even the feeds from social media accounts. Prompt students to access various documents from

around the same time or place that they are working to remember. These texts will not only include useful details, but they might also help elicit more memories.

> ***Technology Tip: Recording and Transferring Files***
>
> There are a number of reminders to consider once you ask students to record materials from the physical world and then transfer them to computers or other web-based digital repositories. As mentioned above, don't assume *all* of your students have mobile devices; be prepared to loan equipment to them. Even if they all do have mobile devices, they are likely to have different equipment (especially camera and audio recording specifications) and data usage plans. Before assigning activities that prompt students to record materials for high-stakes projects, design scaffolding activities that prompt students to learn what their mobile devices can do and how to transfer files to other locations. Remember, don't assume students know where their device stores recorded media or what file type is used.

When encouraging students to use places and things to help remember, assign them to:

1. Keep digital copies of the memory trigger (even if they have to take pictures or record video).
2. Reflect upon each artifact by including:
    - Detailed descriptions of each artifact (put in words what is visible or audible in the digital text).
    - Descriptions of how or why each artifact is important to the memory or event.
    - Descriptions of how each artifact makes the student feel about the memory or event.

Consider prompting students to start a research journal (Learning Activity 4.1) and a digital repository space (a list of possible applications is available in Chapter 4) that they share with you and possibly the entire class.

In the Learning Activities 5.1 and 5.2a/b, you'll find snippets of activities that ask students to find things in the physical world and digitize them. These can be their own activities, or they can be small steps in a larger one. What you'll want to take note of is the prep work sections, as these steps are critical to students taking that digitizing step and making it something useful. There are examples of what it looks like when you assign a particular tech versus having students find and use a tech as well. For an activity like this, the outcomes involve research and digital literacies. You might also use activities like these if you're asking students to do observations or interviews. The focus of the group of activities here is on memory because personal stories are not uncommon in our classrooms.

Learning Activity 5.1 asks students to create a place to store their digitized pieces. We've used Google Slides here, but you could have them create this space in a variety of different programs. The goal is to ensure students have a place to put the things they're digitizing before they actually digitize them. You'll want to do this for all of the 5.1–5.2 activities, even if we don't explicitly build it into the others.

Learning Activity 5.1: Engaging Sensory Details

<h1>Intro Header

<h2>Prepare

<h3>Google Slides

1. Start a Google Slides document in the course's shared folder. Title your document: <LastName>-Sensory-Details.
2. Read/view instructional materials on how to use Google Slides.
    a. **(*Instructor insert: a few recently made documents or videos)**

<h3>Finding things you saw [heard] [smelled] [tasted] [touched]

- For this step, you want to explore your physical surroundings to help you remember an event and specifically focus on the sensory details of that event. You might:
    - go to a place that helps jog your memory or
    - visit that old box under the bed or at the top of the closet.
- Once you've identified the "what," you'll want to:
    - Snap photos of those things. They don't have to be perfect, but make sure you know where the photo lives after you take it and how you can get it to the Google Slides you just created.
    - Spend 5–10 minutes writing words and phrases that describe those things.

>

<h2>Curating

You'll need to add a slide as you continue to collect elements; a slide helps to show and tell what the sensory experience of that memory was. Make sure to add new slides for new senses or when engaging with an additional image or clip. For each memory, include:

1. Your name and a brief title/description (no more than six words) of the memory or experience you are developing.
2. On the slides, paste images of what you saw [heard] [smelled] [tasted] [touched].
3. In the speaker notes, list words and phrases of what you saw [heard] [smelled] [tasted] [touched].

(*Instructor suggestion: We've listed the other senses in brackets, but you'll want to specify to students that you want them to cover each sense, three of the senses, or however you want to structure your activity.)

In Learning Activity 5.1, you might divide it so students are first looking for images of specific senses and then doing a word generation, or you might only have them do one or the other. What matters is that they're being asked to bring the physical elements into the digital spaces so they can both share with the rest of the class and be able to draw on them later. Learning Activity 5.2 has been broken up into "a" and "b" because they're examples of

a. having students select technology themselves and
b. assigning a specific technology.

In 5.2a, make sure students know where to get help because you won't always know how to help them when they're choosing a technology. If it's the first time you're assigning work involving a technology outside of your LMS, you might want to pick the tech for them and explain why you selected that technology as a guide to help them select their own in the future. The pedagogical benefit to having students self-select is its own digital literacy.

Learning Activity 5.2a: Recording Physical Texts—Audio (Student Selects Tech)

<h1>Intro Header

<h2>Prepare

Identify the audio-recording device you will use for this activity. If you are using a mobile device, identify the audio-recording application you will use.

>

(*Instructor insert: Depending on the level of student you're teaching, you might want to provide different options for different operating systems.)

As you're choosing the application, please consider the following questions:

1. Do you have an application on your device already?
2. Does it fit the needs for this assignment?
3. Do you know how to use it?
4. What do you need to know in order to use it?

After identifying what you will use and answering the four questions, go to the web and spend an hour searching for and reading different how-to manuals for recording audio with your specific device and software application. During that hour, also view/read:

- **(*Instructor insert: Provide 2–3 tips/suggestions for recording audio that are appropriate for the project and the course's complexity level.)**

Make sure you know how to convert your audio file into an MP3 and how to move it from your recording device to your computer. **(*Instructor suggestion: This will vary depending on their device and application. This can easily become its own activity.)**

<h2>Record

To legally record people going about doing their own things, you have to do so in a public area (***Instructor note: You may want to prompt students to post a sign stating they are audio or video recording so individuals can choose to avoid the area.**) For this assignment, record audio from one of the following places (you may also propose a different place to your instructor):

- Street corner;
- Public park;
- Public library or museum; or
- Airport (in the general areas outside of security).

Plan to record at least five minutes of audio on three separate occasions at the exact same location. **(*Instructor suggestion: If you are having students take pictures or shoot video, you should suggest they shoot from different angles and locations and change up their shot compositions and lighting.)** You might decide to record the same time on different days, or you might decide to record at different times of the same day. If you record at different times, make sure they are significantly different times (i.e., not just five minutes on and five minutes off).

>

<h2>Reflect

Listen to your different recordings. What are the differences between the separate recordings? The similarities? If you are required to select one recording as the representative sound of this particular location, which one would you pick? Why?

<h2>Submit

- File Repository: In our shared course Dropbox folder, make a file titled "<LastName>-Ambient Audio." Upload your three MP3 audio recordings. Name them: "Location-time-date-<LastName>." Also upload a Word document of your reflection, and title it "<LastName>-reflection-Ambient Audio."
- LMS Assignment: In the LMS assignment area, copy and paste the URL to your specific Dropbox folder.

Each time you have students using programs outside the LMS, be specific about how they should submit their work. Remember when setting the rubric or grading criteria that we suggest you give points for every task you've asked students to complete. For example, the grading rubric for 5.2a would look like this:

Rubric/Grading Criteria

- URL to Dropbox folder (1 point)
- Dropbox folder titled "<LastName>-Ambient Audio" (1 point)
- Three five-minute audio recordings (3 points)
- Each audio recording is in MP3 format (3 points)
- Each audio recording is titled "Location-time-date-<LastName>" (3 points)
- Reflection document titled "<LastName>-reflection-Ambient Audio" (1 point)
- Reflection document includes comparison of similarities across the audio files (1 point)
- Reflection document includes contrast of differences across the audio files (1 point)
- Reflection document identifies one audio file as representative of the location (1 point)

- Reflection document discusses why the one audio file is the best representative text of the location (1 point)

In Learning Activity 5.2b, the application we're requiring has a pretty low learning curve. In addition to what we have here, you might consider creating your own video screencast walk-through that's more contextualized to how your class is using the program. Remember, we're digitally mediating instructions too, and for some students, reaching out for help in an online class doesn't come as easily as asking for help in a face-to-face in-person setting.

Learning Activity 5.2b: Engaging Sensory Details: Recording Physical Texts—Audio (Instructor Selects Tech)

<h1>Intro Header

<h2>Prepare

<h2>Otter.ai

1. Start an Otter.ai account. **(*Instructor note: You can assign any audio recording application that also provides a transcript of the audio text)**
2. Read/View instructional materials on how to use Otter.ai
    a. **(*Instructor insert: a few recently made documents or videos)**

<h2>Record

Use Otter.ai to record yourself talking about the event or memory you want to explore. As you tell the story or talk through the details, try to talk about what you were seeing, smelling, hearing, touching, and possibly tasting.

In both 5.2 Learning Activities, you can ask students to go back to their Google Slides from 5.1 and add the links to their audio to those slides. This can help students keep the digitized texts organized. Remember, at this point students will also want to track in their research journals the "where" ; if they're returning to the same Slides, they can simply put the hyperlink into their journal entries.

Finally, you can ask students to digitize physical texts through video. Just like the activities above, you'll need to decide if you're having students select a technology or if you're mandating one; you'll need to have tech support for how students are going to get it to you; and you'll want to make those decisions based on where they're headed with their pieces. Are those pieces to help them reflect in ways that will become an alphabetic text? Will the project they're working toward be a video? Keeping the end goal in mind helps inform decisions about the smaller pieces and types of scaffolding students will need.

Digital Texts: Alphabetic and Beyond

Productive searching for secondary sources and digital media is best done in two stages. First, your students should carefully articulate what resources they need based on the topic of the project as well as the conventions of the digital production process (see Part 3). In other words, before just sending students out to search for secondary sources or media, be sure they prepare themselves for the search (see Learning Activity 5.3). For example, when searching for digital texts, think about the search terms and other keywords being used to find the texts. Language has bias, in both the good and bad sense of the term, and different words produce different search results. For example, doing a Google image search for "professor" can skew toward specific race, gender, and age groups.

> ***Considering Bias in Language and AI***
>
> An effective way to bring social justice to the forefront of your online literacy classroom is an activity that involves investigating bias. We would argue that AI has actually made this discussion easier as the most popular chatbots at the moment have clearly been biased. There are obvious biases, since the information is based on archives from the freely available web up to a certain date, which we know means that it's using an already biased space to pull its information and its language construction. We would argue that all computer code is biased in one way or another based on the unconscious biases of the programmers. Finally, the prompts that users feed chatbots might also include their unconscious biases which might frame how the application interprets the instructions and produces the results. A conversation about biases AI applications might include is a good moment to both address bias in general and have students discuss affordances and constraints of generative AI. You might do this by having students annotate something the AI generated or investigate the bias of some of the search terms they're using in Learning Activity 5.3.

Prior to looking for digital texts, you and your students might benefit from brainstorming different keywords and getting insights from others (see Learning Activity 5.3). This is particularly important online because it can be more difficult to catch issues with searches and topics without the immediacy of a synchronous in-person space.

Learning Activity 5.3: Preparing to Search for Digital Images

<h1>Intro Header

<h2>Needs Identification

First, identify why you need the image(s). Take some time and answer the following questions:

1. Why do you need the image(s)?
2. What will you do with the image(s)?
3. Based on what you are doing with the image(s), what **licensing** considerations, concerns, or requirements do you have?
4. Based on what you are doing with the image(s), what **content** considerations, concerns, or requirements do you have? What needs to be in the image(s)? What can't be in the image(s)? Are there any privacy or other ethical concerns associated with the content of the images? **(*Instructor suggestion: If you are having students search for information, prompt them to think about the evaluative criteria they will use to assess the relevance, authority, and credibility of the information.)**
5. Based on what you are doing with the image(s), what **formatting** considerations, concerns, or requirements do you have? Size? Format? Shot composition? Angle?

After you have answered those questions, make a requirements checklist that you can use when searching for your image(s). Depending upon the search engine you use, you may be able to filter your results by various licensing and formatting variables.

<h2>Develop Search Terms

Based on why you need the image(s) and what you will do with them, what search terms will you use? What are the core terms you are currently using as you brainstorm, dialogue, and conduct research about your topic? What are synonyms for those terms? Talk to other people; what other terms do they suggest? Have materials that you have read used other terms?

Develop a list of at least ## **(*Instructor insert: Select the number based on the assignment and number of images they need to find)** search terms you will use to find your image(s).

>

<h2>Submit

In your discussion board entry, post your

- answers to the five questions:
    - Why?
    - What?
    - Licensing considerations
    - Content considerations
    - Formatting considerations;
- requirements checklist; and
- **(*Instructor insert: ##)** search terms.

In activities like this, it's useful to have students respond to each other. This is the type of activity where there is no right answer, and so it works better for discussions. We would, in this case, ask students to respond to two classmates without responses and

- specifically engage with at least one answer to the five questions,
- ask a new question or make a suggestion to the checklist, and
- ask a question about their search terms.

We would also assign points for each task we ask students to complete in their responses (so in this case, three points for each response if they did all three pieces in our bullet list).

If you are asking students to find digital texts to use for their own research or projects, we suggest you help them narrow down and focus the research processes. Can you give them search terms and other keywords or help them better articulate their own terms? Can you provide specific locations where they might look for texts? For example, if they are doing research on a specific topic, suggest that they search for resources in topic- or discipline-specific databases, encyclopedias, journals, or trade magazines. Similarly, if they are searching for images, audio, or video to use in a project, provide links to specific search engines and media repositories that are already licensed for reuse (see Learning Activity 5.4). If they are making an infographic about a historical event, you might point them toward library and museum websites.

Learning Activity 5.4: Finding Audio Licensed for Reuse

<h1>Intro Header

(*Instructor suggestion: if you do not pursue an activity like Learning Activity 5.3, you might need to assign a preparation step that prompts students to develop a saving and management process.)

<h2>Search

Based on the results of Learning Activity 5.3 **(*Instructor note: Or based on a set of criteria you assign students),** search the following sites for at least four background music/soundtrack selections you can use for your upcoming video project:

- **(*Instructor insert: at least three different audio repositories)**

<h2>Submit and Reflect

In this discussion board entry, provide functional hyperlinks to the four background music/soundtrack selections you chose. Under each link, briefly describe why and how you think this soundtrack might work in your video.

When creating the rubric for this activity, we want to make sure we're giving credit for each one of those entries we asked for (a hyperlink to soundtrack 1, a discussion of soundtrack 1, a hyperlink to soundtrack 2, etc.). This is important for creating assessment practices that consider time as a social justice issue.

Transitioning Ideas

This chapter is centered on finding and collecting texts. These are the next steps, after organization, for both you and your students before using the texts for a variety of purposes. In the next chapter, you'll read about considerations to make and examples of activities when asking students to read and engage with a text, and the following chapter has considerations to make and examples of activities when asking students to take more robust notes about the reading and annotating they've done on the texts they've found.

Websites and Applications

Creative Commons Search: https://search.creativecommons.org/
Dropbox: https://www.dropbox.com/

EndNote: https://endnote.com/
Flickr Creative Commons Search: https://www.flickr.com/creativecommons/
Google Image: https://www.google.com/imghp
Google Slides: https://docs.google.com/presentation/
Hypothes.is: https://web.hypothes.is/
Mendeley: https://www.mendeley.com/
Otter.ai: https://otter.ai/
PowerNotes: https://powernotes.com/
RefWorks: https://refworks.proquest.com/
TinEye: https://tineye.com/
Unsplash: https://unsplash.com/
Zotero: https://www.zotero.org/

6

Reading, Annotating, and Analyzing Digital Texts

Reading and annotating are key pieces of teaching literacy in our English courses. Making sure we're assigning activities to engage students with the text, with each other, with technology, and with ourselves as their instructors is critical to ensure that the acts of reading, annotating, and analyzing follow our guidelines in this text. We need to be mindful that of all the tasks we assign, reading is a tough one to estimate because reading speed is based on the individual, the purpose, and the text (and we don't just mean alphabetic texts; students might play or replay audio and visual texts at different speeds). Providing concrete tasks to do within a reading can help provide guidance for what students should do with a text in ways that accommodate slower reading speeds and help students stay focused on the purpose for reading. Finally, making sure that the texts we assign and the tools we use to read and annotate have accessible interfaces is paramount for us as instructors.

Reading/Consuming/Engaging Texts

One of the four beliefs listed in the National Council of Teachers of English's (2018) position statement "Beliefs for Integrating Technology into the English Language Arts Classroom" is "Technologies provide new easy to consume and produce texts." Since we now teach students multiple literacies associated with a variety of media, this belief statement reminds us *reading* no longer encompasses what we are prompting students to do. Although we are thrilled to see position statements and scholarship take up the term "consumption," we prefer to use the term "engage" to emphasize that the act of reading or consuming a text is always engaging with ideas and meaning making. In other words, we want to teach students they never simply read/consume a text, but they should always be engaging with a text, which benefits from actions like highlighting, annotating, and note-taking.

We acknowledge that literacy instructors are already knowledgeable and experienced in designing learning and assessment activities around

>

reading and meaning-making. However, like Schmidt and Kruger-Ross in *Reimagining Literacies in the Digital Age* (2022), we believe many literacy instructors desire support in helping students engage with multimedia. Both the changing modalities of the digital texts as well as the new functionalities of the digital engagement applications provide new opportunities for designing critical engagement activities with and for students. As with the suggestions in *Reimagining Literacies in the Digital Age*, our suggestions for designing reading/consuming/engaging activities are likely to feel familiar while introducing or invoking a few digital twists.

In this chapter, we start by discussing the importance of mindful reading and how we frame that to students. We know mindful reading/engaging is important in all modalities of literacy instruction; however, we emphasize it here because of the complications with instructions in asynchronous online courses. Specifically, we highlight the need to develop engagement frameworks or guidelines in order to provide students with detailed, operationalized instructions for when they are reading on their own. We then shift to practical application with activities and concrete suggestions for reading, annotating, and analyzing in digital environments. We suggest that building frameworks helps students read, annotate, analyze, and synthesize (Chapter 7). That's not news, of course, but in digital spaces, frameworks are important for supporting engagement. The texts students analyze might be ones the instructor provided, ones students found, or ones students collected as part of a primary research process. The activities in this chapter build upon one another but use a variety of different engagement frameworks and technologies to show how you might adapt the whole set for your needs. Each activity can be adapted for the media types students will be asked to use. To help you connect activities together, we note elements that are expected to have already happened for each activity.

When considering our guideline for social presence in reading, annotating, and analyzing primary and secondary texts, consider offering students space to share their analyses in what can otherwise be an isolating experience. It will be important, however, to balance additional requirements to create presence with the need to value students' time. Remember that students in online classes are often short on time; this means making the engagement activities worth their while. Finally, tools, technologies, and methods should be accessible to all students. They'll also need scaffolding to help learn the technology in order to complete the engagement activities.

Analysis versus Synthesis

For us, and in this book, analysis is when you focus on and study a specific subject. You might analyze an article, book, or film; you might also analyze a focused group, like books by the same author or answers to the same interview questions. Analysis usually means breaking things into parts to understand how and why they work. For our purposes, synthesis means comparing and contrasting different objects in order to make meaning. This sounds a lot like that last sentence in analysis, doesn't it? Obviously, these are fuzzy distinctions; however, one of the easiest ways to understand the difference is by conducting research.

- **Analysis**: Reading individual articles found as a part of secondary research; possibly producing an annotated bibliography with the results.
- **Synthesis**: Comparing and contrasting articles from secondary research, identifying trends and themes, and then weaving together a review of literature.
- **Analysis**: Carefully reviewing observations of the same location at different points of time. Identifying different trends and categories of how to break up and understand what information is present. (Yes, this is the fuzziest one!)
- **Synthesis**: Comparing and contrasting information from secondary research with data from primary research to tell a story of what we learned.

One of the ways we like to distinguish analysis from synthesis is by emphasizing systematic review when doing analysis. Synthesis, on the other hand, leaves more space for brainstorming and exploration as a way to see different connections between and across materials.

Documenting and Managing the Process

Before you prompt students to read, annotate, and analyze texts, we want to briefly remind you (as introduced in Chapter 4) and your students of the importance of keeping a research journal or set of research memos. At every point in the process, your students will be making decisions about what questions to ask, what data to collect, how to process texts, and what they think about all of this. Having students track the entire process is important—and, as with everything else we suggest, digital journaling can be a useful, multimodal process. As you saw in Learning Activity 4.1, we suggest prompting students to start a journal, diary, or set of memos early in the project and that you periodically check in on them. Hopefully, they'll quickly learn that you can't direct them regarding all the points they should and will want to take notes on. Visit Chapter 7 for more ideas about detailed, multimodal note-taking, but at this stage in the process, make sure students have updated reflection questions (i.e., that they are not just using the original template you made them). For example, you might shift your reflection prompts in Learning Activity 4.1 to be:

- What did you just work on?
- Where is it located?
- Where are your notes?
- Did you get stuck? If so, how did you persist?
- How does what you did connect to previous work on the project?
- What surprised you about this work?
- What did you learn from this work?
- What work do you need to do next?

Facilitating Mindful Reading, Listening, and Watching with Frameworks

When we're teaching in online spaces, we're assigning these activities within digital spaces using digital tools. Two decades of research shows people read online alphabetic digital materials more quickly than print materials (Moran, 2020). We also know that an affordance of some video and audio programs is the ability to speed up the clip. When assigning reading and annotating activities in digital spaces, then, we need to adapt our methods to encourage students to engage with the text in a way that fits their purpose for reading (Cohn, 2021).

Online educators must design activities that facilitate mindful reading. Mindful-reading assignments ask students to carefully and critically engage with the text. For example, Cohn (2021) suggests teachers assign reading engagement activities that prompt students to do one of the following: curate, connect, create, contextualize, or contemplate. In other words, asking students to engage with multimedia texts in carefully constructed ways helps them learn. When designing a mindful online reading activity, we work from two assumptions and one fact:

- Assumption #1: Everyone reads texts with a specific purpose.
- Assumption #2: Everyone is more likely to understand and remember the text if they actively engage with it.
- Fact: Many digital reading/consuming applications (including audio and video) allow readers to mark up and annotate digital texts.

Whatever level we teach, we can't assume students know how to do the critical work of identifying targeted or thematic frames to help with reading. Prior to assigning students to read texts, you'll want to identify or help students articulate the reasons they are reading the text.

For example, when having students read texts to help with a research project, you might suggest they identify and comment upon the text's thesis or claim, reasons, evidence, research methods, and conclusions. Frameworks in literature analysis might include characterization, setting, narrative conflict, etc. For rhetorical analysis, your framework would include purpose, audience, author, evidence, and rhetorical moves; for a genre analysis, your framework would involve content conventions, format conventions, language conventions, and adaptations/deviations. How these frameworks are developed depends on your goals in the course. If a specific goal of the course is to become independent critical readers, you'll want to require students to step back and think about what they want or need to gain from their reading. Prompting students to create a framework for reading can help them shift from thinking about what they need to developing a plan for how to execute their reading and research. Helping students shift from thinking about what they need to creating a plan means assigning students to create a framework for reading. A reading framework should center on providing structure to their reading processes and should be an assigned scaffolding step before they are asked to read. Consider having students workshop their reading frameworks with one another.

However, if you are teaching new content or a new framework to students, you should provide a reading framework as part of your job in teaching the content. They are new to the content, and they need help identifying what is important. Regardless of how the reading framework is developed, consider having students share their texts after they've done the highlighting or annotating step. They'll see that not everyone focuses on and makes meaning from the same details. Sharing and comparing will also provide a reason for students to spend more time with the text. Learning Activity 6.1 provides the structure for how you might have students work together to build a framework for the class to use. The examples we give in the instructor suggestions for Learning Activity 6.1 are to illustrate how we might adapt this activity if we were using it for a research project.

Learning Activity 6.1: Building a Framework

(*Instructor suggestion: When this activity happens in a physical space, you can circle the room to make sure everyone is doing the brainstorming; when not in the same space, those checkpoints have to be built into the activity design.)

<h1>Intro Header

<h2>Read

- **(*Instructor insert: Your own content/textbook readings on using articles in a research project.)**
- **(*Instructor suggestion: We recommend having secondary or college students spend no more than 45–60 minutes reading for this activity and suggest that you articulate a limit.)**

<h2>Write

(*Instructor suggestion: We suggest that before you have students come together to build the framework, give them time to brainstorm a list of questions based on the type of framework they're building. For example, if you're assigning a research project, you might have students brainstorm questions about:

- **thesis/claim,**
- **reasons,**
- **evidence,**
- **research methods, and**
- **conclusions.**

You'll also want to be specific about how many questions students should be generating.)

<h2>Add

To our group document, please add your list of questions. Be sure to include your name before the list or highlight and add a comment to the list so we know which questions are yours. **(*Instructor suggestion: When having students work in collaborative digital documents, provide guidelines on how they can clearly articulate the work they did.)**

>

<h2>Comment

(*Instructor suggestion: Here, we suggest you tell students to comment on the collaborative document. Again, you need to be specific—we would assign students to comment on three potential questions. Also be sure you link to "how-to add comments" support materials for the particular word processor you're using. Finally, one of the most difficult aspects of asynchronous discussions is crafting the instructions so that the interaction is meaningful. We suggest giving students specific elements to focus on in their comments. For example, you might ask students to focus their comments on whether or not they feel like the questions would help them find the framework elements in a piece.)

<h2>Submit and Reflect

After you've added questions and commented on your classmates' work, please copy and paste the URL to our shared doc in this assignment folder with a reflection on how the activity helped you understand what you'll be looking for in your sources. **(*Instructor insert: Name of the project this is working toward. If we stick with the example above, this would say "research paper.")**

(*Instructor suggestion: When assigning work in digital spaces, tell students where we're looking for the work. We recommend keeping this as consistent as possible and sticking to the place where you're entering grades—typically, your LMS. It's also useful to help students connect what they did to the course trajectory by asking them to reflect on how they'll use the work moving forward.)

<h2>Rubric/Grading Criteria

Highlighting

Whether in print or digitally, highlighting texts we're reading is easy—almost too easy. If designed as an activity to help read the text, highlighting can be extremely useful. Guided highlighting can help students spend finite amounts of time in processing the text, and it can help students critically focus on specific elements of a text.

Why Highlighting Frameworks?

We've all seen, or maybe been guilty of ourselves, texts where there is lots of highlighting on the page without anything else present to help make meaning.

One of the benefits of reading digital alphabetic texts is the ability to easily highlight with a rainbow of colors to help articulate meaning or to mark up a video, an audio track, or an image. Identifying sections of a text is the first step to analyzing it. When students first read something, you might assign a targeted or thematic framework with each element associated with a different color or code to guide highlighting in meaningful ways.

Technology Toolbox: Highlighting and Annotating Applications

- Kami
- Hypothesis
- Perusall
- Adobe PDF Reader
- Filestage
- PDF Annotator
- PowerNotes
- Timelinely

Continuing with our research example from the last section, after you've helped students establish the framework for conducting research, you might suggest that they identify the text's thesis/claim, reasons, evidence, methodological or philosophical framework, research methods, and conclusions. If you are having students read texts as a model of a particular genre, you might have them identify specific content and structural conventions across a few samples. If students are reading literature, they might highlight sections that develop a character, show narrative conflict, or describe the setting of a scene. If students are highlighting to understand and translate a complex topic, you might have them highlight and articulate critical points of understanding. A benefit of assigning digital texts is that students can write on it without worrying about "ruining" their hard copy or having to pause and take handwritten notes about a movie.

In addition to needing a framework to help them identify evidence for their particular purpose, students will also need frameworks to identify meaningful pieces of the text. You can help students identify why they are reading the text and then use that purpose to develop questions to ask about the text so that students can approach texts with focus. In our example about reading texts for research, questions someone might ask could include:

- Why were these authors writing about this topic?
- Who were the authors writing to? Why that audience?
- Why are these authors authoritative and credible?
- Why is the data/evidence authoritative and credible?
- How are the authors making their point?
- What is their point?

Simply highlighting the text only has students identify important sections; answering questions about it causes students to analyze what they think is happening, why, and where the text helps make meaning. Do you remember a time you went back to a reading you highlighted and annotated but struggled to figure out what your past self was thinking? We remember all too well. For example, in Figure 6.1, you see the solid blocks of yellow highlights, and then one with blue and yellow highlights. The multicolored highlights help us chunk the information, but what does it mean? In our image, the point is not for you to read the text; it is an example of what coded highlights might look like.

You can help students avoid this by prompting them to develop highlighting and annotating guides or keys for their frameworks. Creating a key that identifies what each color means will help their future selves remember the framework. For color-blind students, you could also suggest adding a keyword from the framework for each highlight.

Why We Need Framework Codes

In a highlighting assignment, make sure the student provides a key for what each highlighter color or icon represents. For example, Figure 6.2 shows the key for the blue and yellow highlighting in Figure 6.1.

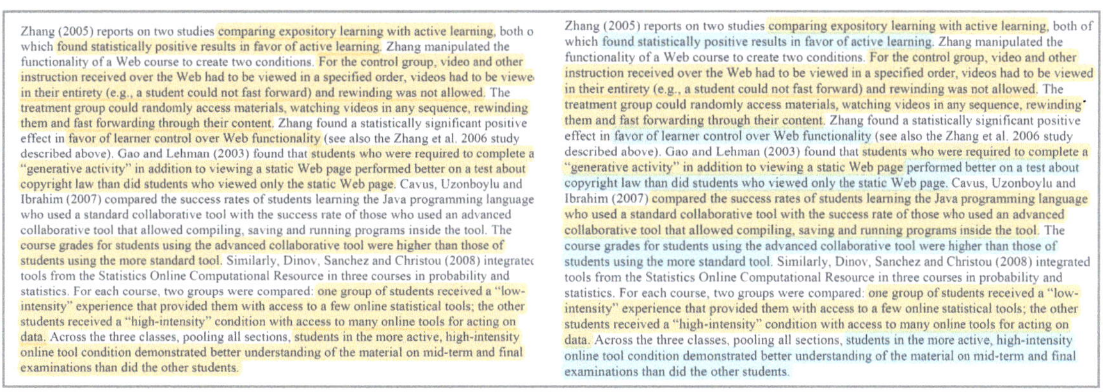

Zhang (2005) reports on two studies comparing expository learning with active learning, both of which found statistically positive results in favor of active learning. Zhang manipulated the functionality of a Web course to create two conditions. For the control group, video and other instruction received over the Web had to be viewed in a specified order, videos had to be viewed in their entirety (e.g., a student could not fast forward) and rewinding was not allowed. The treatment group could randomly access materials, watching videos in any sequence, rewinding them and fast forwarding through their content. Zhang found a statistically significant positive effect in favor of learner control over Web functionality (see also the Zhang et al. 2006 study described above). Gao and Lehman (2003) found that students who were required to complete a "generative activity" in addition to viewing a static Web page performed better on a test about copyright law than did students who viewed only the static Web page. Cavus, Uzonboylu and Ibrahim (2007) compared the success rates of students learning the Java programming language who used a standard collaborative tool with the success rate of those who used an advanced collaborative tool that allowed compiling, saving and running programs inside the tool. The course grades for students using the advanced collaborative tool were higher than those of students using the more standard tool. Similarly, Dinov, Sanchez and Christou (2008) integrated tools from the Statistics Online Computational Resource in three courses in probability and statistics. For each course, two groups were compared: one group of students received a "low-intensity" experience that provided them with access to a few online statistical tools; the other students received a "high-intensity" condition with access to many online tools for acting on data. Across the three classes, pooling all sections, students in the more active, high-intensity online tool condition demonstrated better understanding of the material on mid-term and final examinations than did the other students.

Zhang (2005) reports on two studies comparing expository learning with active learning, both of which found statistically positive results in favor of active learning. Zhang manipulated the functionality of a Web course to create two conditions. For the control group, video and other instruction received over the Web had to be viewed in a specified order, videos had to be viewed in their entirety (e.g., a student could not fast forward) and rewinding was not allowed. The treatment group could randomly access materials, watching videos in any sequence, rewinding them and fast forwarding through their content. Zhang found a statistically significant positive effect in favor of learner control over Web functionality (see also the Zhang et al. 2006 study described above). Gao and Lehman (2003) found that students who were required to complete a "generative activity" in addition to viewing a static Web page performed better on a test about copyright law than did students who viewed only the static Web page. Cavus, Uzonboylu and Ibrahim (2007) compared the success rates of students learning the Java programming language who used a standard collaborative tool with the success rate of those who used an advanced collaborative tool that allowed compiling, saving and running programs inside the tool. The course grades for students using the advanced collaborative tool were higher than those of students using the more standard tool. Similarly, Dinov, Sanchez and Christou (2008) integrated tools from the Statistics Online Computational Resource in three courses in probability and statistics. For each course, two groups were compared: one group of students received a "low-intensity" experience that provided them with access to a few online statistical tools; the other students received a "high-intensity" condition with access to many online tools for acting on data. Across the three classes, pooling all sections, students in the more active, high-intensity online tool condition demonstrated better understanding of the material on mid-term and final examinations than did the other students.

FIGURE 6.1. Highlights Done by Authors on Page 41 of Dept. of Ed 2010

In an annotation assignment, you might ask students to code their annotations. For example, the following research-related questions might be coded with:

- Why were these authors writing about this topic? (AUTHOR-PURPOSE/ Yellow)
- Who were the authors writing to? Why that audience? (AUDIENCE/ Green)
- Why are these authors authoritative and credible? (AUTHOR-CREDIBLE/Blue)
- Why is the data/evidence authoritative and credible? (EVIDENCE-CREDIBLE/ Pink)

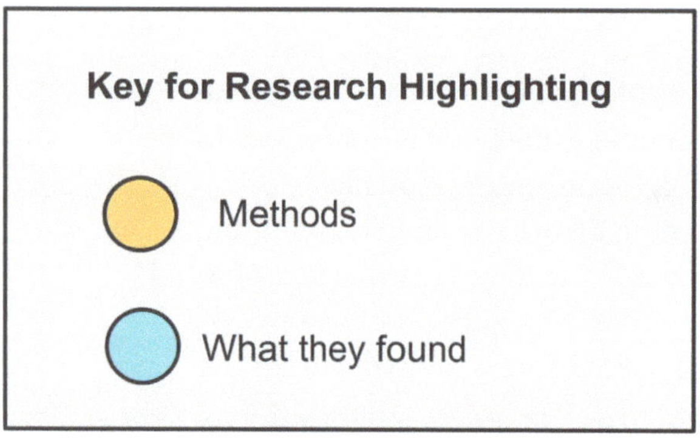

FIGURE 6.2. Key for highlighting framework

In the assignment instructions, you would ask students to highlight using the assigned colors and, if they use annotating features (discussed in the next section), to start each comment with the appropriate ALL CAPS CODE so that it is easy to sort specific answers.

These keys and codes will make it easier for you to quickly skim student work to check if they completed the assignment. More important, keys and codes make it easier for all students (including those with visual impairments) to go back and reference specific sections of their text when reading and replying to each other or when cross-analyzing with other sources.

After highlighting the text, a comparison of color-coded highlights across readers can be a powerful activity. If all students were given the same text and the same color code key/framework to use, their resulting texts should look similar. However, the differences and the discussions about why and how the choice to highlight a specific section was made will lead to learning. The actual colors are less important than the codes, and this practice of letting students choose their own color codes makes your course more accessible to color-blind students.

> *Selecting Accessible Tools*
>
> Although we love multimodal texts, we are, at heart, word nerds. As such, the development and distribution of the vast array of applications allowing users to engage with and produce alphabetic texts in so many ways—some beyond what can happen in print versions—excite our technologically mediated hearts. And we have found many students are excited about the various functionalities that allow them to play with what they are reading and learning. However, some of these creative functions are not necessarily great tools for diverse users. How well does an application work with a screen reader? How well is the application designed in terms of readability and visibility? What cultural assumptions drive engagement with the app's interface or functions? We leave this accessibility reminder here, between talking about digitally highlighting and annotating, to remind you to think carefully before selecting an application that all students must use. Before basing an entire lesson plan or assignment sequence on a specific application, be sure to test it with a variety of users. In sharing this concern, we also admit it is one of the reasons we tend to provide a few choices of technologies to our students for many projects; however, we also admit when it comes to reading, annotating, and analyzing a document, we usually require the same application because we want students to be able to share documents and engage with one another. For example, Catrina had a blind student who requested to use the technologies that they knew well and that worked with their screen reader instead of the assigned application. The answer was a resounding yes, of course, but there are no easy choices as an instructor selecting technological applications.

Annotating

Annotation is a useful tool when trying to synthesize prior learning with what's currently being learned, and it's also useful when helping students understand why they're highlighting text. In order to have students use annotation to synthesize a text and move ideas forward, you'll want to consider using an annotation tool that allows students to comment and, literally or figuratively, draw connections. Ask students to use highlighting and questioning to make connections between specific concepts they've already learned (like identifying an author's ethos) and what they're currently reading (like how the author builds that ethos). Annotations can be done in conjunction with highlighting and in multiple rounds to point to a specific focus of that round of annotations. And like highlighting, you can prompt students to use annotation frameworks to help them analyze texts and organize their thinking. Keep in mind that frameworks and annotating are also helpful in trying to understand primary data students have collected themselves. For example, if you have students collect personal data or observation data (like the examples provided in Chapter 5), frameworks and annotations are ways to analyze that qualitative data.

Annotating Alphabetic Text

The first time a student reads through and annotates a digital text, focusing on analysis is a productive method. To make that round of annotation useful, you'll want to guide your students through what exactly they're analyzing and where they might find those pieces. The identification of aspects of a text to analyze is critical to understanding how to annotate the text in ways that will help students connect the text to what they're supposed to be learning or gleaning from that text.

This identification might be an extension of or an addition to the frameworks in the highlighting section, and it is something that students might want to take notes on or question. For example, in keeping with the running example in this chapter, if students are reading a text to analyze for use in a research project, after they highlight, they might question or take notes using that same framework:

- Highlight the purpose. Then, indicate how this demonstrates the purpose or question what the purpose is if it's not clearly stated.
- Identify the audience through highlighting. Then, take notes on the text about other potential audiences not clearly stated.
- Highlight the text for the credibility of the methods/evidence. Then, take notes about questionable areas of credibility and how the methods might be useful in students' own research or how the methods might be improved.
- Identify the authors' point. Then, take notes on how that point might be useful in students' own research.

This first round of annotation is often best done on an individual basis, as it gives space for students to interrogate the text and have something to share. We also want to be sure that students are annotating a single text at a time. When assigning individual annotating assignments, be sure you have students annotate for a specific purpose like understanding sources, genre, or rhetorical situations. For this section, we provide a detailed example through rhetorical analysis because, as a framework, it requires finding information and taking notes external to the text, which is covered in Chapter 7.

Finding Rhetorical Elements in Digital Spaces

When students are analyzing articles or websites, the contextual information they're usually looking for is not always on the surface and therefore might not be an object they can highlight. For example, books have copyright pages, and most journal articles include the title, volume, issue, and year information on the first or last page. On websites and personally produced and distributed videos, students sometimes have to dig for the author or the audience. Some ways to help students find specific contextual pieces of a digital artifact are as follows.

- **Author/ethos:** When searching for information about the credibility of an author, have students check the "about me" or "about us" sections, which can help them determine who exactly is behind the work they're evaluating. They might also want to search for information about specific authors, publication venues, and/or publishers to find out more information to help assess authority and credibility.
- **Audience:** The audience of a piece is sometimes highlighted in the publisher information. For an online academic journal, you might need to send students to the publication information page and ask them to find the "Aims" or "Scope" section in order to locate the readers of that particular journal. For pieces that are not journals, this information can often be found in the "About" section of a site. Sometimes students will need more precise guidance on specifically identifying the elements of the piece that might point to who the intended audience might be.
- **Dates:** With digital publications, instructors will want to differentiate between published dates and modified/updated dates. Published dates are often easiest to find. Modified dates can be found in the html code of a page (there are different steps to finding and accessing the html code for different browsers; once there, search for keywords like "modified" or "updated") or through resources that search for metadata on a site for you like the one from WebNots: HTTP Header Checker. There are many other ways to check dates (like cache dates, which indicate that something was updated).

These are not all of the contextual elements students might struggle in identifying; for example, if a student just finds a PDF of an article, they might not realize it is from a journal. Further, some company or nonprofit websites, especially those that post blog entries or articles, might look and feel a lot like the website of a digital publication site for a magazine or trade publication. When looking for contextualizing information, students will want to take notes about them in a variety of ways by journaling and keeping track of the elements within the source tracker or citation manager.

Annotating Alphabetic Text to Collaborate

Speaking about a text helps with learning, and when using digital texts, we can start those conversations directly on the text itself. Traditionally, we annotate alone because we read on our own and make marks on a text in ways to help ourselves make meaning. However, digital texts allow for collaborative annotations, which can help to alleviate some of the issues with reading online texts that cause us to miss information (Moran, 2020). Collaborative annotations also allow students to create social presence that is critical in creating a Community of Inquiry (as discussed in Chapter 3). That doesn't mean students should not first do an individual round of processing with highlighting and annotating; in fact, if you're introducing a new concept, giving students space to read individually can help them be better prepared to be collaborative in useful ways. Regardless, collaborative annotation tasks need to have clear guidelines and goals in order to be effective.

Before you outline what layers of prompting you will share, first consider the process in which students will collaborate.

- **Collaborative Annotation Applications:** Some applications allow multiple students to annotate the same text, including: Hypothes.is, Perusall, PowerNotes, and Kami.
- **Passing Files:** While not ideal, your contextual constraints might require that students pass a file back and forth for collaborative annotation. If so, make sure they are using the same application or they might not be able to see their classmates' work. You might also provide suggestions for document titling conventions that include initials, dates, and times.

Having students code their annotations in the same way they coded their highlighting will make it easier to organize and continue the dialogue in future assignments. If the annotation application does not automatically stamp each annotation with an author's name and date/time stamp, make sure you include instructions for students to at least add their name and date to each new annotation.

A layered, collaborative annotation assignment might necessitate that:

1. You provide students with a highlighting framework and color key to identify pieces in the text. Consider breaking students into groups to focus on specific sections of the framework or sections of a longer text.
2. Students ask each other questions to create a discussion about why those pieces were highlighted with that framework element color. You'll want to identify how many questions to ask. You might also want to provide example questions and codes for specific types of questions.
3. Students read and reply to one another's questions.

If your assignment has layers like above, you will likely want to break up the work over a few different due dates so students aren't stressed about waiting on classmates to post their work. Remember, online students are often fitting classwork in among other responsibilities that might be a higher priority for them.

Annotating Audio and Video Texts

The highlighting and annotating frames and suggestions used earlier also apply to audio and video clips. What changes is the how and the where of those activities due to the nature of those types of texts. When annotating audio and video clips, just as we ask students to identify by highlighting alphabetic text, we want students to highlight the audio or video file first. The easiest way to do that is to work in time stamps, as it's a visual/text-based queue to the information that is being "highlighted" in those types of files. When assigning audio and video time stamping, you'll want to be specific about how many minutes of audio/video you want your students to view/listen to. The highlighting frameworks suggested earlier can then be applied to the time stamps that students create in their audio and video clips.

The logistics of time stamping and annotating can be as low tech as opening up a word processor, typing the time stamp, and typing your annotation for that highlighted moment (using the annotation frameworks outlined earlier in the chapter). However, if you're comfortable supporting more involved technologies (or comfortable saying, as we do, "thanks for playing with this new tech with me!"), then a lot of free options exist that have specific functionality to make these processes easier. The functionalities you want to look for are the ability to time stamp and to add an annotation to that time stamp. Ideally, those annotations could be in a variety of modalities: text, audio, video, and image. Then you can prompt students to use a variety of modalities to complete those annotations.

Learning Activity 6.2: Annotating Video

<h1>Intro Header

(*Instructor note: This assignment assumes you have had students sign up for an account at Timelinely, your class has created an observation framework, and your class has gone through and added cards to the videos students are observing. These cards should have students type out the code color word or put an image of a solid color to help them in the highlighting activity. Note that this is the necessary process because color-code functionality is not available in Timelinely at the time of this writing. And we use Timelinely here because, again at the time of this writing, it is the only free video annotation tool with a low learning curve.)

<h2>Read

Spend no more than 45–60 minutes rereading:

- **(*Instructor insert: your own content/textbook readings relevant to the goal of annotating)**
- Your **(*Instructor insert: type of framework you're having them use here)** framework and questions created in a previous activity

Rewatch:

- Your video where you tagged your time stamps with our framework color coding in the previous activity. **(*Instructor suggestion: This assumes you've already had students go through and "highlight" time stamps.)**

<h2>Annotate

Return to your Timelinely video and add video/audio/text/image annotations to your Timelinely cards. You are required to complete at least three Timelinely annotation cards. Each card must include: **(*Instructor insert: What exactly they will be annotating for in this activity.)**

(*Instructor suggestion: When asking your students to annotate video, we suggest you remind them of the framework and guide them toward the goal of the activity. For example, we imagine annotating video for the purpose of observation. If that was our goal here, we'd ask students to remember that we want to add to the observation framework we built as a class by keeping what they're seeing and what they think about what they're seeing separate.)

>

<h2>Submit

Click "Publish," and then copy and paste your link into this assignment folder. With your link, please include a reflection on what you learned from **(*Instructor insert: What exactly they were annotating for in this activity)** and how you'll use this in your project.

<h2>Rubric

Submission includes:

- URL for Timelinely (1 point)
    - Timelinely activity includes at least three cards (3 × ***Instructor insert: Number of points for each card with breakdown below** = 3 × # points for all the cards) with annotations that include:
        - **(*Instructor insert: What you asked students to include in their annotations)**
- A reflection (1 point)

(*Instructor note: We built out this rubric to show how nuanced we would make the rubric based on the details we're asking students to produce. If we were to ask students to complete an observation here, for example, we would add: What you saw [3 points], and What you think [3 points] as rubric items.)

Annotating Personal Information

In Chapter 4, we discussed how your students might collect memories or artifacts representing memories of previous people, places, or events. Some of the strategies provided to help students recall these memories also start basic analysis procedures by systematically organizing memories. The activities here push analysis beyond just remembering details to connecting to thoughts, feelings, and reflections.

Sometimes, analysis in personal information might include further exploration and uncovering of details. In other words, the act of remembering is analysis, and while doing analysis, your student might also remember more. The suggestions for how to remember and generate details in Chapter 5 emphasize systematic exploration of memories as a way to collect information. That emphasis on an orderly progression is what makes them both personal data collection activities as well as analysis activities.

However, students might use additional activities to analyze their previous experiences. In these analysis activities, systematically distinguishing between what happened and why it happened is helpful. Analysis can also focus on what happened and how it made the student (or someone else) feel and why that event triggered that feeling. Since these details have been digitized, students can use highlighting and analysis frameworks on this kind of information as well—the framework will just look a bit different. For example, if you ask students to investigate the memory details they pulled together in Learning Activity 5.2b, you might then have them create a highlighting and annotating framework that looks at the following:

- Why it happened
- How it made me feel
- Why I felt that way
- Useful evidence for my narrative

Assigning steps like this can help students imagine different ways to break up the details of their information.

The majority of projects requiring a lot of student-generated memories and details result in narratives. Another way to analyze personal details is assigning them different aspects of a narrative arc (Learning Activity 6.3). Asking students to plug their memories into a narrative arc might also help them identify their claim or point to the narrative.

Learning Activity 6.3: Mapping Memories to a Narrative Arc

<h1>Intro Header

<h2>Prepare

(*Instructor insert: For this activity to be successful, students should have a clear understanding of a narrative arc and its various sections. Ideally, the instructor has provided instruction on narrative arcs and provided examples using 2–3 stories that the entire class is familiar with.)

>

<h2>Map of Narrative Action

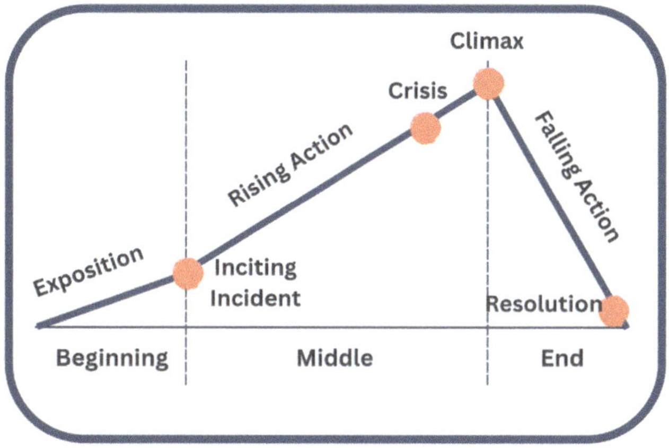

FIGURE 6.3. Map of Narrative Action

<h2>Describe

In a separate word-processing document, describe the details from your memories for each section of the narrative arc depicted in the Map of Narrative Action (Figure 6.3).

- **Beginning**: What was the normal situation prior to the events? Who were the main characters? What were their normal activities?
- **Inciting Incident**: What event occurred that disrupted the norm? What went wrong? What was the problem?
- **Rising Action Incident #1**: On the path to trying to solve the problem or return everything to normal, what was one incident that either pointed the way or blocked the path?
- **Rising Action Incident #2**: On the path to trying to solve the problem or return everything to normal, what was another incident that either pointed the way or blocked the path?
- **Rising Action Incident #3** (if needed): . . .
- **Crisis**: What was the final crisis point where the problem was fixed or the story ended?
- **Climax**: How was the problem fixed?
- **Resolution**: What was the new normal?

>

<h2>Submission

1. If you complete your visual as a drawing by hand, take a picture of your visual. Once your visual is digital, title the visual's file: LastName-NarrativeArc-Visual
2. Title your description file: LastName-NarrativeArc-Description
3. Submit your documents in the course assignments area.

(*Instructor suggestion: First, we suggest students submit their documents in a space where they can see one another's work. Most will be unsure of their analysis and will want to compare it with others. Second, you could easily add a peer-review activity in which you prompt students to give feedback on one another's narrative arcs. For example, suggest that students leave at least three who, what, when, where, why, or how questions in the description document.)

<h2>Rubric/Grading Criteria

(*Instructor suggestion: We would break this into two categories—visual file and description file—so students are earning completion credit for each small piece they turn in. Be sure to give credit for each task.)

Another way to analyze memories is similar to what we suggested for students annotating and taking notes on digital texts. Students should first focus on the claim, focus, or point of their personal story. They can then carefully reread through their notes and highlight the details that are required to make the point or claim of the narrative. Once students have identified the required details, they can then go back through the work and identify whether other details are necessary for the story.

Transitioning Ideas

Throughout this chapter, we articulated the "why" for breaking down the highlighting, annotating, and analyzing processes into discrete steps, how you might approach each step, and ways to do it outside of traditional individual text-based work. These ideas, activities, and tools point to a few things we need to remember. We need to:

1. Work with students to create strategies for mindful reading for specific purposes.

2. Give structured activities that guide students through the highlighting, annotating, and analyzing processes so they are focused and productive when they do this work.
3. Provide or help students develop frameworks for analyzing the texts they are reading.
4. Provide students with other ways to do this work (collaboratively or with multimedia applications).
5. Scaffold the technology. When introducing students to a new technology, show or tell them how to sign up, find resources, and do the steps in the activity that you want them to complete.

After all this reading and analysis, students then need the space, time, and tools to synthesize information.

As we wrap up this chapter that has focused on gathering and understanding information from reading, we transition from ways to start organizing that work to ways students can begin to synthesize and then use the information they've gathered to support their own learning.

Websites and Applications

Adobe PDF: https://acrobat.adobe.com/us/en/acrobat/pdf-reader.html
Filestage: https://filestage.io/
Google Docs: https://www.google.com/docs/about/
Hypothesis: https://web.hypothes.is/about/
Kami: https://www.kamiapp.com/about-us/
Open Office: https://www.openoffice.org/why/index.html
PDF Annotator: https://www.pdfannotator.com/en/aboutus
Perusall: https://perusall.com/about
PowerNotes: https://powernotes.com/
Timelinely: https://www.timeline.ly/about
WebNots: HTTP Header Checker: https://www.webnots.com/seo-tools/http-header-checker/
Word 365: https://www.microsoft.com/microsoft-365/word?rtc=1

7

Synthesizing Digital Texts

Now that you've found your texts (or had students find them; Chapter 5) and asked students to highlight and annotate individual texts (Chapter 6), we suggest that you distinguish between annotating in the text and pulling notes into a note-taking space for synthesis. Here, we discuss ways of synthesizing notes in a systematic way that enables students to remember, reuse, and reflect upon the content in a more robust and sustained manner. The first section of this chapter transitions from Chapter 6 by focusing on the logistics for taking notes outside the texts themselves. In this section, we offer next steps, ensuring that these always jibe with what you've done previously. The logistics should neatly fit together in ways that don't cause cognitive overload. The second section of this chapter focuses on the types of notes students might take outside of the texts and capitalizes on digital spaces to help students make progress on the process.

Before we get started, we want to remind you that one of the greatest affordances of taking notes in digital environments is the ease with which students can share their notes with you and their classmates. Again, we focus on digital environments because online students are already in digital spaces but also because those sharing opportunities help students create social presence. Whether taking notes and then getting feedback or taking notes as a collective, digital note-taking applications usually allow for robust collaboration. Although some of the activities in this chapter might not explicitly prompt it, we want to remind instructors that it is easy enough to add instructions for students to take and share notes, read and comment upon one another's notes, revise and add to notes, comment again, and then rinse and repeat.

Taking Notes outside the Text

In addition to the annotations that students may take on the text, as in Chapter 6, students often need to take notes outside of the text. These notes typically fall into two categories:

1. external to the content of the text but specific to the individual text, and
2. synthesis work that might be throughout a single piece or across pieces.

Be transparent with students about why returning to the annotations to pull them into synthesis work or doing extra digging into the context of the text are key practices. Especially in online accelerated courses, students can see taking the time to do these as discrete steps as "busy" work. Explaining the purpose can go a long way toward getting students on board.

Before they start the notes external to the text, remind students that one of the affordances of having done their annotations digitally is that the frameworks they developed or used with those previous tools can help them take those external notes and start synthesizing. As we know, it's not always cut and dried, but reminding students they've created the digital threads they can add to in order to weave their stories is worth doing.

Logistics: Where and How to Take Notes

Once you have helped students identify the frameworks needed to take notes about their texts (see Chapter 6), you'll also want to provide suggestions regarding where and how to take their external notes. These decisions need to be made early because they impact all types of note-taking that students will do, not just directly on the texts they're working with. You might already have students working in a space where they can easily take notes related to the individual texts as well as to start synthesizing what they're seeing across threads; if not, then making sure those spaces are easily integrated with the other annotating and writing work students are doing is key.

Multimodal Note-Taking

We suggest asking students to use a variety of media and modalities to continue taking notes. The examples below are suggestions for helping your students create that network between the text and the notes they're taking. Sometimes, it's a direct link (embedding, recording, hyperlinking), sometimes it's pulling bits out for reference (transcribing, copying and pasting, taking photos), and sometimes it's creating a hub for doing all the additional note-taking work (creating digital noteboards and whiteboards):

- **Transcribe**: The oldest method of taking notes is to transcribe the text. This, however, usually only works well with alphabetic texts. Prompting students to audio record themselves reading a text might be useful so they might repeatedly listen to the text. Even if the text already has an audio option, sometimes the power of transcription is the act of the student making the text their own through their own writing or speaking. This type of space can be used for external notes or for synthesis notes, and it is useful for situations where you're trying to ease the digital load while taking advantage of digital spaces. For example, you might even prompt students to make a handwritten transcription of a text and then take pictures of their handwritten notes. Don't forget, once students start trying to transcribe audio/visual material into words, it becomes interpretive; however, they can also take pictures and record mixed media as a form of transcription.
- **Copy and Paste**: Again, with digital texts, students can obviously copy and paste alphabetic text. It is now easy to copy and paste other modalities as well (like graphs in a text). On the one hand, having an extra copy of something to annotate and otherwise mark up is always helpful. On the other hand, make sure students remember copyright is a concern and making a new "copy" is potentially breaking copyright laws. Copying and pasting is another lower-learning curve method that gives students space to use tools they're more familiar with, but it also doesn't take full advantage of current digital tools.
- **Take Pictures**: Closely related to copying and pasting is taking photos. This can be done with physical texts (students can use mobile devices) or digital texts (students can take screenshots of alphabetic text, images, video stills, or transcriptions). This is another method that gives students a way to connect the text or piece of a text they want to other digital resources, but like the others, would still need a "home base" like Google Docs.

Practicing Accessibility

We find that students get frustrated with producing accessible texts in the same way they get frustrated by producing stylistically correct bibliographic citations. In other words, once they are done producing the core project, they don't want to spend even more time polishing it. When you prompt students to produce multimodal notes, you might also prompt them to practice producing accessible texts: use heading formatting features so that

>

a screen reader can more easily navigate the text. If including an image, produce alt text for the image (e.g., they should already be typing up the text for the handwritten note example mentioned above). Instead of copying and dumping long, ugly URLs into the notes, take a few extra moments to format the URL as hyperlinked readable text. And, in case you are worried about this taking more time for you to assess and provide feedback, prompt students to review and provide feedback on one another's accessible adaptations.

- **Hyperlink**: If the text is digital, always make sure students' notes include a hyperlink to the original file (whether it is on the web, in a database, or on their hard drive). Even if students make or download another copy, be sure they link to the original. This is one of the easier ways to make sure students are connecting notes to the text when they go beyond annotations.
- **Record**: Are your students making observations or conducting interviews? If so, have them digitally record the experience, making sure they have permission from interviewees or people in the pictures or videos. Consider having students audio or video record their own thinking and note-taking processes. Since some free, or more affordable, transcription applications like Otter.ai are available, it's worth requiring students to always auto-transcribe audio or video texts at the very least.
- **Embed**: Depending on where and how students are taking notes, they might be able to embed images, audio, and video into their notes. Embedding is like linking, but it allows the reader to see the file being linked. Embedding is useful because it does not create another copy (which potentially breaks copyright).
- **Digital Noteboards and Whiteboards:** Sometimes it helps to take notes in an environment that allows the student to visually organize their thinking. You might consider having students take their external notes in a place where they'll be taking their synthesis notes (see the next subsection in this chapter).

The key here is connections. Working in digital spaces allows us to move, shift, and connect texts and notes in ways that should be systematic, and planning the "how" enables us to help students stay organized and use the affordances of digital spaces without becoming overwhelmed.

Noteboards and Whiteboards

A number of note board or whiteboard applications now exist, many of which have templates that can help students take notes. Many of these applications also allow you to make a template board that your students can then copy and complete as part of their note-taking assignment.

> ***Technology Toolbox: Noteboard and Whiteboard Applications***
>
> - Cardsmith
> - Conceptboard
> - Draft
> - Hoylu
> - Miro
> - Padlet
> - Stormboard
> - Trello

We sometimes request our students to try different applications or different templates within the same application as a way to figure out what note-taking structures work best for them and their current project. We then ask students to both share notes and share reflections on the different note-taking applications and frameworks.

External Note-Taking Frameworks

Some texts (and authors) have a larger network of texts that contribute to its meaning and significance. For example, after students watch the full-length feature film, you might ask them to research and take notes on:

- the director (or other key figures in the film or part of its production),
- reviews about the film, and
- scholarship about the film.

Similarly, if students are reading an article from a newspaper or a trade magazine, they might want to find other publications by the same author or information about the publication venue. (See Chapter 6 for a refresher on the types of frameworks that prompt students to collect notes about a text externally.)

The larger network can also apply to genres and can help students understand how their text fits in that larger context. The design and conventions of a text might require taking external notes about the design and conventions of a specific genre that the text falls under as well as how the text conforms to and differs from the larger genre conventions.

Format and Design Notes

When texts are online, we often call their formatting their design. Taking notes about the design of a document, a video, an image, or an audio clip that already exists can be tricky in online spaces. Instructing the student to carefully articulate what aspect of the formatting or design they are analyzing becomes critical. With alphabetic texts, having students reference the page number might not be enough direction for the notes they're taking. For example, you may want to ask students to reference the location on the page: "page 10, upper right-hand corner." Similarly, students can reference time stamps in audio or video texts as well as specific sections of the shot composition in a video.

As mentioned earlier, when analyzing the format or design of a text, we need to prompt students to take advantage of the digital environment and include pieces of the text they are analyzing like:

- Cropped images from a page,
- Cropped elements of an image,
- Cropped still shots from a video, or
- Short clips of an audio file.

In short, when asking students to take notes on format and design in digital environments, remind them that notes can be more than just alphabetic text.

Jigsaws

In addition to supporting individual student work, noteboards and whiteboards with sharing capability work well for creating community in digital spaces and for breaking up the labor, especially if you're teaching a course or module that needs to move particularly fast. We never have enough time to teach all we hope to. Jigsaw activities, though potentially complex, allows students to split the labor, teach someone else, and learn from each other, which in turn strengthens your learning community. We reference jigsaws here because they bridge note-taking and synthesis. Students first individually take external notes particular to a reading or learning session in order to become an "expert"; they then collaboratively synthesize with classmates in both "expert" and "teaching" group sessions.

What Is a Jigsaw Activity?

A jigsaw activity is when instructors break students into groups for students in each group to become experts on a specific topic (Group A, Topic A; Group B, Topic B, etc.). The instructor then reshuffles the students into teaching groups so that each group has one expert for each topic (Group 1 includes at least one member from Groups A, B, C, etc.; Group 2 also includes representatives from Groups A, B, C, and so forth). The second-round groups do the synthesis work of combining together the learning from each of the separate topics.

Jigsaw activities can be a really effective way to build in group work online without the pressures of high-stakes group activities. However, in online classes, you'll need to be very explicit about who puts what notes where. Structuring the jigsaw so that you're providing the collaborative space, the framework, the readings, and dividing up the work can help these activities run smoothly. For example, in order to help students better understand a reading, you might divide the reading into themes and assign each group member a particular theme to report on. You might ask students to then use the collaborative note board space to teach the rest of the group about their themes. Alternatively, you might break students into groups of three, assign three different readings about the topic, and have students report back to their classmates about what they learned. Whichever way you decide to structure the activity, in online spaces, monitor activity so that groups with members who are not engaging might be reorganized. If that reorganization can't happen, which is particularly common in accelerated online classes, it will be important to structure the activity in a way that the groups can also share with each other; this is why it's important that you are the one who creates the digital note-taking spaces.

Synthesizing Information

We define synthesis as comparing and contrasting information to identify trends and themes that tell a story. That story might be to articulate a problem, to articulate a need or a question that needs to be answered, to support a claim about how a problem might be solved, etc. When asking students to synthesize their notes for online courses, help students identify what they're trying to accomplish in the synthesis and then find the tool that will best help them accomplish that goal. Sometimes, students can use the same tool, and sometimes they need to select a new tool to get the work done. The synthesis stage is also when you are likely to ask students to compare, contrast, and synthesize information from both primary data and secondary sources.

In this section, we focus on weaving as our framing. The finding, reading, and annotating in Chapters 5 and 6 set students up to start synthesizing what they know in order to begin telling the stories. Any external notes they've taken will help them tell those stories. They've collected the threads to start pulling together and will now need to take their notes and start bunching the threads into groups to be woven together. In this section, we focus on steps and methods for the synthesis process:

- Reflecting
- Organizing Methods
- Synthesis Methods
    - Visual Textual Analysis
    - Digital Note Spaces
    - Spreadsheets

Which method students use will depend on the project, how much support they need, what tools they're using already, and what their preferences are. However, regardless of how you ask students to synthesize, the most important component is reflecting on their synthesis work.

Reflecting

When synthesizing notes students have already taken, make sure students are reflecting on the process and their decisions as they go. This reflective work can be attached as part of any synthesis assignment or required as part of their research journal process (see Learning Activity 4.1). When teaching synthesis in online courses, it's critical to remember that students will need guidance on the steps that we might normally go over in a classroom and will need assistance in selecting the best method for their goals. You will want to provide similar assistance during their reflective process. Robust reflection notes are a part of their synthesis work, and in many cases, pieces of research reflection can be used while writing up the results of their research project.

As you continue to have students add to their research journals, have them consider the following questions when they reach the organization and synthesis stage:

1. Describe the work you just completed. What steps did you take?
2. What major decisions did you make? What criteria did you consider in making your decisions?
3. How does what you just completed connect to the research work you have already completed for this project?
4. What do you need to do next? Why these next steps?
5. Did you have any problems or issues while you worked? What did you do, or what will you do, to overcome them?
6. What information did you learn or generate?
7. What surprised you? What alarmed you?
8. How do you relate to what you have completed or learned? (Saldaña, 2021, p. 69)
9. What patterns, categories, themes, and concepts do you see emerging in your research? (Saldaña, 2021, p. 69)
10. How does what you completed help you answer your research question and complete your project?

If you're using Learning Activity 4.1 as a starting point, these questions would go under step three of "Write/Add." Or based on a specific analysis or synthesis activity, you might give students specific questions to answer.

We want to conclude this section on reflection by reminding you that reflection need not only be completed using alphabetic text. Consider prompting students to find images that represent what they are thinking or learning and find a snippet of music to represent how they are feeling during their learning and production processes. Prompting students to complete audio and visual reflections will provide low-stakes experiences for them to play with and experience the fuzzy correlations between ideas and their concrete external representation through things such as different words, images, colors, sounds, instruments, etc.

Organization Methods

At this point, students have annotated on their texts and have taken external notes related to the contexts in which their texts function. Next, students need to organize what they've learned and they've read across multiple individual texts. When setting students to this task, the frameworks that you or they created early on become incredibly useful. Students can apply those themes or concepts across texts in order to begin making connections between texts and ideas. These framework elements can give students a useful way to synthesize what they have learned.

For example, students might have highlighted and annotated two or three sources and found information on the backgrounds of those sources (establishing their ethos). In an activity that asks students to organize and synthesize what they learned from their sources, you might ask students to revisit the frameworks they've been working in to start putting evidence or ideas from each source into "buckets" as a next step to drawing connections between the sources. As an alternative, you might ask students to establish the topics they know they want to cover in their projects as the points of organization. The key here is to prompt students to take what they've done and begin organizing it in order to then synthesize the ideas. At this point, they don't need to draw the connections; they just need to parse out what they have.

We know synthesis is a key step in any writing or composing project. However, in online spaces, when students are working with texts that are multimodal and when notes are scattered across digital spaces that can't physically be put next to each other, clearly emphasizing each step will help keep them from getting lost in the digital spaces in which they're working. Some tools make this process easier than others (for example, tools like PowerNotes provide the space to build a framework, highlight, annotate, and synthesize texts and images). Carefully consider how tools work together to help students in these processes.

Referring to Media in Organizing Notes

In the same way you can copy and archive resources in a variety of modalities, think about how students reference media within their notes. When referencing parts of visual media, students might want to crop portions of an image or a screenshot so that the combination of their written and visual notes stay focused to a specific element. Similarly, when referencing specific sections of linear media (e.g., books, audio and video files) students should use common markers like page numbers or time stamps.

At this point, if you've had students highlight/annotate on the videos and images, you'll want them to focus on pulling those previous notes into a space where they can synthesize and expand upon the ideas in ways that help them make critical connections. For example, if you were asking students to understand the conventions of a children's YouTube channel, you might ask students to use the annotation and highlighting tools on a series of videos from that channel. After doing that work, the next step is bringing those notes into a single space. This space might be as simple as a Word document; however, what students will need while learning in digital spaces is guidance on what to pull in from their annotations, how to track the themes they're seeing, and what evidence to collect that points to these themes. One way we might start to do this is to ask students to take screenshots of the videos and record time stamps for elements that can't be captured in a static image. These "quoted" pieces are the chunks of evidence that students are collecting. As students collect, they should continue to use naming conventions for files (like screenshots) and articulate what the time stamps mean to the purpose of the project they're working on.

Synthesis Methods

Making meaning from primary data and secondary sources is an extremely complex and difficult process. We find it is helpful to provide students with a variety of creative options to help them play with the information they have collected to explore what new ideas, themes, and meanings emerge.

Visual Textual Analysis

Before we introduce some digital visual analysis applications, don't forget that doodling and drawing is sometimes the easiest way to have people explore connections between the content, materials, and ideas with which they are working. Giving students the freedom to use colored pens, pencils, or crayons and scratch paper can generate lots of connections. It's usually easy to ask students to snap pictures of their doodles and upload them to an LMS submission area.

Automated Analysis

A number of textual analysis and visualization applications are available on the internet that allow you and your students to quickly analyze and visualize data about a text. We are big fans of word cloud generators to get a quick sense of what words are used the most in a given text. Some word cloud generators provide the numbers of each word present in the text. Some web applications like WriteWords have both word and phrase frequency counters. These basic text analysis applications will allow you and your students to quickly identify important trends in the text based on word and phrase frequency. You can then use digital find functions to identify exactly where these common (or rare) words and phrases exist in the text for further analysis. You might encourage students to compare and contrast results of frequent words and phrases across various texts (both secondary sources and primary data like interview transcripts and answers to open-ended survey questions). Identifying and comparing word and phrase frequencies might help students identify core concepts and themes across their primary and secondary data sources.

Student-Created Cluster or Mind Maps

Visually grouping together concepts, ideas, sources, and data and then drawing connections between them is a creative method for synthesizing information. Some activities might emphasize making the connections between content (Learning Activity 7.1). Connecting or networking activities usually helps students develop a narrative or line of reasoning about the larger meaning emerging from the content.

Learning Activity 7.1: Mind-Mapping Content

<h1>Intro Header

(*Instructor suggestion: To ensure that students identify both the associated ideas and the connections between them, we suggest you select a digital application that at least requires connections between nodes—possibly one that even forces hierarchical connections. Even if the student has to reject a connection, leaving a node as a complete outlier, the application will have made their need to do so explicit enough to help understand the meaning being made.)

<h2>Prepare Mind-Mapping Document

1. Go to Bubbl.us and look at the Mind Map examples so you understand some of the ways you can display and connect nodes.
2. Start a Bubbl.us account and make a page.

<h2>Prepare Your Thinking

Review all of the materials you have collected and already written for this project. Skim through your notes and content.

<h2>Draft Your Mind Map #1

Start mind-mapping your research or project as you currently understand it. Consider making and connecting nodes for:

- common themes or specific concepts;
- research questions or lines of reasoning that support a claim; and
- details from secondary sources and/or primary data.

>

Take advantage of using colors, font, and formatting of lines to differentiate types of nodes and connections. Be sure to start a legend where you keep track of what a specific color or other formatting feature means.

<h2>Revise Your Mind Map

Wait at least two days before revisiting your project information and mind map again. Skim all of your project materials again. Revisit your mind map. Make alterations to the mind map and your legend.

<h2>Submit

1. Save your mind map as a jpeg file. Name it "LastName-MindMap"
2. In a word-processing document, type up your legend and include the picture of your mind map; title the document "LastName-MindMap-Legend"
3. Upload both the word processing and jpeg documents to the assignment area.

<h2>Rubric/Grading Criteria

Remember that for activities like this, you'll want to give students points for uploading the pieces you want and what those pieces should contain (for example, a point for each node you require). Although a number of digital applications allow for cluster and mind-mapping, sometimes hand-drawing or working with index cards or sticky notes is easier for students. When done, they can quickly digitize the results of their mapping by taking pictures and sharing the images with the class.

Digital Notecards

Physical notecards (or sticky notes) can become ideas that you can move around to help you synthesize information. In digital spaces, students can reimagine those cards in a variety of ways that mimic the ability to stack cards on top of each other or move them next to each other.

In Learning Activity 7.2 is an example of how students might synthesize the notes they have so far. As mentioned in the External Note-Taking Frameworks section earlier in this chapter, students might have already started pulling information into a note board, so now they just need to organize it and start to draw the connections between the ideas. Some noteboards allow greater flexibility in moving notes around, so when choosing a note board, be sure to consider how you want students or how those students plan to use it. The example in 7.2 allows students to create cards that can be moved around anywhere on the board they would like, which can assist in just getting the ideas down on cards before moving them around. Any program that allows for space to create notes students can move around would help with this part of the synthesis. As always, considering whether you're going to require the same program or let students pick a program is your first choice. Learning Activity 7.2 uses the program Conceptboard and assumes students have already worked in it before this activity.

Learning Activity 7.2: Synthesizing Your Note Board

<h1>Intro Header

<h2>Read

Reread your notes in your Conceptboard from Activity **(*Instructor insert: Specify the assignment that asked students to take notes in the board)**.

<h2>Sort and Stack

1. Post your research question in a large font or different-colored note at the top of the board.
2. Take the sticky notes you created in your Conceptboard for Project 1 and sort them. You can do this by dragging and dropping notecards into piles. As you're grouping your sticky notes, start thinking about the ways the ideas and notes you took previously work together. What commonalities do the notes have in helping you answer your research question?
3. Make sure you have at least three separate piles. In other words, try to push yourself beyond any plain binaries like "for and against." Even if you have two major pro/con categories, look for themes within each category; you'll likely find different groups of reasons that individuals support or argue against an issue.
4. After you've piled your notes, separate each pile out a bit so you can see what's on each note. Then, click on the line/arrow tool to start drawing the connections between the note piles that you've made. Create a new sticky that summarizes the ways these ideas connect for each note pile.

>

<h2>Reflect

Spend twenty minutes or so writing a reflection about how each pile summary will work to answer your research question. How will the first pile transition to the second pile and work together to set up the third pile? How will these piles of notes work to help answer the question? What did you learn by grouping your notes together this way?

<h2>Submit

In your Conceptboard, make sure you click the blue share button in the right corner, select the Access tab, toggle on link sharing, and copy the link. Submit your Conceptboard link and your reflection to the assignment folder.

Some students (and projects) work better with linear notecards. These students might struggle with organization, and these projects might be straightforward with regards to required organization. Again, some places where students might already be taking notes provide that functionality. For example, in PowerNotes, students can bookmark texts, create digital notecards that are attached to quotes or images, and create notecards that help make transitions between ideas. Students can then drag and drop notes wherever they make sense in a linear order. If students are using the same program, like PowerNotes or in the spreadsheet example below, you'll want to make sure to include the "Return to" step in your instructions that then have students work on synthesizing.

Spreadsheets

Spreadsheets, like Google Sheets or Microsoft Excel, give students the space to start seeing patterns and making connections.

Technology Tip: Working in Spreadsheets

Spreadsheets function differently than word-processing documents. If you are going to ask students to do work in spreadsheets, we suggest you take time to teach them some of the core elements of how a spreadsheet works. At a minimum, make sure they understand the distinction between rows and columns and how to identify a single cell by its column letter and row number. If you are going to ask students to format text and use hyperlinks, be sure to teach them how to make those changes as well.

Spreadsheets can be particularly useful if students are struggling with the synthesis or categorization of their data. If the project you've assigned has specific framework elements that students are looking for, you can give students the categories in which they should synthesize each example or object. For example, let's say you're asking students to conduct a rhetorical analysis, and you've had them annotate the piece they're analyzing and take notes about what they found based on prescribed elements. If their next step is to analyze more examples, you might then provide them a spreadsheet with the following categories in the first row across the various columns:

- Purpose
- Audience
- Evidence
- Author
- Rhetorical Moves

Students can then annotate the actual examples and add the information for each example across each row in the spreadsheet. This will ultimately allow the student to compare and contrast their notes from all the examples; see a genre analysis example in Learning Activity 8.1 (Chapter 8). If students are synthesizing for projects where the categories or themes are not given to them, then they will need to create those elements themselves through the themes they learned from previous annotating activities. If students have more freedom in developing criteria for synthesis (this usually occurs when all the students are completing different research projects and have different themes or trends to compare across their secondary and primary sources), then you can encourage students to add their own categories or themes to synthesize as they're reviewing their notes (see Learning Activity 7.3).

The list of criteria, themes, or categories can become the rows or columns students will synthesize across. Students will then put their notes from each source across the opposite axis. The benefit to spreadsheets is that this can be another sheet in their workbook, so they're continuing to work in the same digital space. For example, you might ask students to start a spreadsheet to track secondary resources they collect, as with Learning Activity 4.2, and then start a second sheet in the same file to conduct note-taking, analysis, and synthesis work, as with Learning Activity 7.3. Some complex note-taking programs, like PowerNotes, will even automatically generate spreadsheets for students.

Learning Activity 7.3: Synthesizing with Spreadsheets

<h1>Intro Header

<h2>Prepare Spreadsheet

1. Open a Google Sheets document and title it "LastName-Synthesis"
2. Make the following column headers across the first row of the document:

    1 Title of Source (or Author and Year of Publication)

    2 Full Bibliographic Citation (or Detailed Description of Primary Data Source)

    3 Summary

    4 Theoretical Framework

    5 Research Methodology

    6 Research Idea/Concept/Theme #1

    7 Research Idea/Concept/Theme #2

    8 Research Idea/Concept/Theme #3

    9 Research Idea/Concept/Theme #4

    10 Other Notes

    11 Source Analysis

(*Instructor suggestion: You may want to make a template document or spreadsheet that students can use to make copies and start their own documents. See the Learning Activity 7.3 tab in the Secondary Research Note-Taking Spreadsheet example.)

	A	B	C	D	E	F	G	H	I	J	K
1	**Focused Topic/Research Question:**										
2	**Title of Source (or Author & Year of Publication)**	**Full Bibliographic Citation**	**Summary**	**Theoretical Framework**	**Research Methodology**	**Research Idea/Concept/ Theme #1**	**Research Idea/Concept/ Theme #2**	**Research Idea/Concept/ Theme #3**	**Research Idea/Concept/ Theme #4**	**Other Notes**	**Source Analysis**
3	Source #1										
4	Source #2										
5	Source #3										
6	Source #4										
7	Interview										
8	**Synthesis**										
9											
10											

FIGURE 7.1. Example of Secondary Research Note-Taking Spreadsheet

QR 7.1. *Secondary Research Note-Taking Spreadsheet* Provide students with a spreadsheet in which they can take organized notes: https://tlo.pub/spreadsheet

<h2>*Input Information*

In each new row, input information about each secondary source or piece of primary data (e.g., interview, observation). Remember, these are your notes based on your analysis of the source or data. You can add brief quotes, but most of the language should be your own.

You should include at least four rows/entries about different secondary sources and one row/entry representing at least one interview.

<h2>*Synthesize Information*

1. In the last row on the bottom, add the term "Synthesis."
2. Carefully read each column of information. In the synthesis cell at the bottom of each column, add your synthesis about what you see across all the sources and pieces of data.
3. In the last column on the right, add the term "Source Analysis."
4. Skim across each row of data. In each source analysis cell, add information about how this source or piece of data connects to other specific sources or data and/or connects to the synthesis notes at the bottom of the spreadsheet.

<h2>*Submit*

Copy and paste the URL into the assignment submission area of your project's Google Drive folder.

<h2>*Rubric/Grading Criteria*

- Google Sheet titled "LastName-Synthesis" (1 point)
- URL to Google Sheet submitted in submission area (1 point)
- Row at the top includes the ten column headers listed above (10 points)

>

- Four complete rows of information about four separate secondary sources (10 points × 4 rows = 40 points)
- One row of information about an interview (10 points)
- Complete column of source analysis notes (5 points)
- Complete row of synthesis notes (10 points)

Please note that Learning Activity 7.3 is worth a lot of points; however, it is prompting students to do a lot of intellectual work. We've built this rubric because this particular type of work is time consuming for students, and so giving points for completing each piece is important. This may be an activity you break up over time—for example, by asking students to complete one row of information each night for homework or prompting them to spend 60 minutes each night and then finish the analysis and synthesis work on a final session. In other words, asking students to do all of this in one sitting is likely to lead to an incomplete spreadsheet.

Once you have seen a synthesis spreadsheet, you are likely to imagine ways to develop your own frameworks based on a specific assignment. The point is to provide students with a systematic way to take notes on individual objects and then compare and contrast the notes about each object.

Transitioning Ideas

Although this chapter rounds out the section on Reading, Viewing, and Engaging with Texts, we're writing teachers at heart. We know students should be writing or otherwise recording as they are reading, thinking, and learning so they already have text prepared when they start to produce their own texts. The information that students have learned, materials they have collected, and ideas they have synthesized will prepare them to produce a variety of texts suggested in Part 3. In the first chapter of Part 3, Chapter 8, we assume you already have activities you're doing to help students write alphabetic texts. What we then offer in that chapter are suggestions for shifting that process online.

Websites and Applications

Bubbl.us: https://bubbl.us/
Cardsmith: https://cardsmith.co/

Conceptboard: https://conceptboard.com/
Draft: https://draft.io/
EndNote: https://endnote.com/
Google Docs: https://www.google.com/docs/about/
Google Sheets: https://www.google.com/sheets/about/
Hoylu: https://www.hoylu.com/
Miro: https://miro.com/
Otter.ai: https://otter.ai/
Padlet: https://padlet.com/
PowerNotes: https://powernotes.com/
RefWorks: https://www.refworks.com/
Stormboard: https://stormboard.com/
Trello: https://trello.com/
WriteWords Word Frequency Counter: http://www.writewords.org.uk/word_count.asp
WriteWords Phrase Frequency Counter: http://www.writewords.org.uk/phrase_count.asp
YouTube: https://www.youtube.com/

III

Teaching the Production of Texts

In Part 3, we provide detailed suggestions for having students use digital applications to produce both traditional texts and genres as well as multimedia texts and other creative genres. We outline considerations when crafting an assignment prompt and the grading criteria, then we provide a discussion of and activities for scaffolding the process of creating different types of text, which includes:

- Designing the Instructions
- Scaffolding
  - **Teaching the Conventions**—Students and instructors are more comfortable producing and assessing in new genres and media if the assignment process and grading criteria include careful attention to conventions, affordances, and constraints.
  - **Teaching Preproduction**—Writing studies traditionally uses "invention" to describe brainstorming and other prewriting activities. Preproduction work includes all the activities in which students do the thinking and planning for their project.
  - **Teaching the Technologies**—Teaching in digital environments highlights the need for instructors to explicitly build in steps, lessons, and activities that help students learn the technologies they will use throughout the production process.
  - **Teaching Revision and Polish**—Finally, working in new media with new applications can be overwhelming. Both instructors and students benefit from having specific examples prompting students to revise and polish their texts before final submission.

8

Alphabetic Texts

We imagine that you and many of your students already have plenty of practice producing alphabetic texts in digital environments. We imagine large parts of our audience also have plenty of experience prompting students to write in digital environments. This chapter will function as a template for the remaining production chapters while also serving as a reminder of things to consider for an audience already experienced with (teaching the) digital production of alphabetic texts, especially when teaching online asynchronous courses.

Students are often most experienced in using alphabetic texts as a way to create social presence in the online classroom. It's the most common type of text they peer review. However, in considering the time constraints our online students have, we need to make sure that we're creating activities that give them the time to create the spaces and use the technologies we're asking them to use, even in alphabetic text. Finally, we need to make sure that what we ask them to do is accessible, like we repeat in every chapter in this book, but also that they consider how their work is (or isn't) accessible.

Designing the Instructions

Although it may feel like the conventions of traditional, hard copy, alphabetic textual assignments have not changed because of the shift to both digital production and consumption processes, small changes have snuck in. Now that it is easier to include images and hyperlinks in predominantly alphabetical texts, more and more instructors are asking students to do so. As a result, even popular genres are shifting; instead of asking students to write a story about what they did last summer, you might ask them to produce a listicle of what they learned last summer. Now that it is easier to format alphabetic texts, instructors are asking students to be more aware of design, accessibility, and usability issues like using headers and providing alternate tags for images and tables.

With both the internet to find media and genre examples as well as many word-processing and other production technologies to provide templates, the process of students producing texts that look like they follow the conventions of a given genre can be even easier. Let's take résumés as an example. Résumés have started to become a bit more diverse because of the ease with which authors can include images, hyperlinks, and formatted text. Students can also easily find examples to copy or templates from which to work. This doesn't necessarily mean, however, that students understand the what, how, and why of different parts and sections and formatting choices in résumés. You, the instructor, still need to teach them that. In fact, because of the ease with which students might find and copy digital examples of texts, you providing detailed scaffolding activities is even more important to ensure students are producing their own materials and instruction about the genre conventions they'll be using and the rhetorical choices they'll be making (see Learning Activity 8.1, "Finding and Analyzing Examples").

As with traditional alphabetic text assignment prompts, providing students with the rhetorical situation (both the learning one in which they are participating for a grade as well as any contextualized one for which they are producing) is helpful. In other words, major project assignment instructions benefit from having:

- Purpose
- Audience
- Learning Objectives
- Process Steps/Outline (these may be on the major assignment prompt, or they may live in your course as activities you ask students to complete during the module or unit)
- Submission Guidelines (see Major Project Excerpt 8.1)
- Rubric or Other Grading Criteria

When teaching textual production in and through digital technologies, two of these categories require a little more nuance: process steps/outline and submission guidelines. At a minimum, you need to build in steps that teach students to use the applications for producing, workshopping, polishing, and sharing or submitting their texts. Just because you know your students have been using word-processing applications, do not assume they know how to insert headers, make hyperlinks, or format hanging indents. Similarly, how exactly do you want the digital text submitted? In what format? Using what file-naming conventions? And, especially in the later chapters, you'll also realize your grading criteria will account more for elements like design and digital delivery.

Major Project Excerpt 8.1: Submission Guidelines

<h2>Submission Guidelines

For the final draft of this assignment, please title your project "Last Name_Project #_Class_Semester/Year" and submit as a **(*Instructor insert: identify file type)** to the assignment folder in **(*Instructor insert: identify the LMS you are using)**.

While we anticipate that you have grading criteria specific to alphabetic text already, you'll want to make clear your grading criteria for digital submissions of alphabetic texts as well. Major Project Excerpt 8.2 has some criteria you might add to what you have.

Major Project Excerpt 8.2: Grading Criteria

<h2>Grading Criteria

(*Instructor note: These are criteria specific to alphabetic text, but you may also use criteria listed in Chapters 9, 10, and 11 for multimodal texts.)

- Document follows organized file naming conventions (e.g., LastName_FinalProject#1_SemesterYear)
- Document titles and section headings are formatted using the word-processing heading setting feature
- The submission is 700–1,000 words
- The submission includes all of the following at the top of the document: a title, your name, the date, the class section number, and the assignment name
- The submission is a story about the author focused on literacy
- The submission focuses on a specific literacy experience
- The submission includes description/reflection regarding the significance of the experience
- The submission provides a reason, evidence, and details to support the significance/claim/thesis
- The submission provides a clear organizational structure to the project (usually chronological)

>

- The submission uses at least two *narrative* patterns of development
- The submission includes detailed sensory descriptions of people, places, and things
- The submission includes a brief conclusion or ends with a motivating idea

Scaffolding

Of course, asking students to write the prototypical term or research paper is not much different from when students were prompted to write it in pencil and paper or on the typewriter . . . or is it? Although the scaffolding processes to help students find, analyze, and synthesize the information and ideas they'll use in their writing have generally remained the same, they have gone digital (revisit all of Part 2 for descriptions of how). Therefore, all of the students' thinking and writing is already in a format they can simply copy and paste from their thinking and learning activities to start producing their writing activities. Consider telling students before and as they do note-taking, analysis, and synthesis work that they are generating materials they'll be able to use to start writing their paper. Also consider assigning students an activity in which they copy and paste relevant elements of their note-taking, analysis, and synthesis work into a single document as their zero draft.

Teaching the Conventions

Before having students mash up the preproduction work you had them produce from activities in Part 2, asking students to carefully analyze examples of the genre and media to identify the conventions they'll want to use when producing their own text is helpful. Depending on the level of the course, you might provide the examples or ask students to find examples to analyze and share.

Learning Activity 8.1: Finding and Analyzing Examples

<h1>Intro Header

<h2>Read

(*Instructor insert: Include five examples of the genre you're asking students to write in.)

>

<h2>Write/Add

For your initial post, select three of the five examples above. For those three samples, identify the following elements:

- rhetorical situation
- language conventions and patterns
- design features
- organization
- content
- style

Keep track of what you've found in a table that allows you to compare the areas across all three samples in order to look for similarities you can identify as conventions. For example, you might do this:

Sample	Rhetorical Situation	Language Conventions	Design	Organization	Content	Style
1						
2						
3						
Similarities across all three						

<h2>Post and Reflect

Post your table with a one-paragraph reflection on some of the must-have elements for this type of genre.

<h2>Respond

Respond to two classmates, focusing on one element they found to be a convention of the type of project we're working on.

Because we use completion rubrics, we would assign a total of 24 points, which includes seven points for all the focus areas for all three samples, plus one point each for the reflection and each response. This suggestion is aligned with our theme of time and social justice because this activity can be cognitively challenging for students, it takes varying amounts of time based on experiences and challenges, and they are producing observable pieces. You might also consider making this a jigsaw assignment (review Chapter 7 for jigsaw ideas).

Teaching Preproduction

Even when asking students to write a story from their imagination, instructors know the story will include more rich details and be better developed if students are asked to generate ideas and focused pieces of the text. In Part 2 of this book is a variety of examples of preproduction activities you would likely ask students to complete while producing an alphabetic text, and the chapters include activities to help students carefully read, annotate, take notes, analyze, and synthesize from published texts, collected data, their own experiences, and the world around them.

Unless otherwise explicitly prompted, much of the resulting information and reflections students developed while completing preproduction activities is often in written, alphabetic format. A common step in producing media is to identify and collect the required materials needed to produce the audio, video, or image. Usually the research, analysis, and synthesis phases during a traditional alphabetic writing project already produce the materials needed to draft the alphabetic text. As we've mentioned previously, we assume most English instructors already have outlining and drafting activities they might assign to students when producing a written text. We envision those drafting activities as useful for introductions, outlines of various types, or sections of the piece like the results or discussion of a research paper. The goal is to have students build the text piece by piece. This is incredibly important in online courses, especially asynchronous ones where students will benefit from a guided and scaffolded process so they don't try to do the entire project in one sitting.

Teaching the Technologies

When teaching things like video or website production, our need to teach how to use the production technology is obvious. Don't forget that assuming students already know how to do something with more commonplace technologies like a word-processing application is always a bad idea. This is especially important when considering our students for whom English is an additional language. If students are struggling with English, yet all of the instructions are in English and the program they're using is in English, then those students may struggle. Word processors can also have a different interface when using them in a different language. Interfaces also function based on *common* cultural assumptions (i.e., common to those with privilege); these are probably not the same assumptions of all our diverse students. While the goal of your course is to teach literacy, leaving the technology in the background puts some of your students at a disadvantage.

Making sure students have found and can use some of the basic document set-up elements is useful at the beginning but also when having students create a reference page. This is partially because the places where those functions live can be different depending on the program you're using (or when you did your last program update). You'll need to decide if you're going to have students use all the same program or if students will have a choice before adapting the assignments below to fit your context. An assignment that prompts students to prepare document formatting, like Learning Activity 8.2, should become commonplace for technical communication courses.

Learning Activity 8.2: Start Your Document

<h1>Intro Header

<h2>Read/View

(*Instructor insert: Videos or how-to documents for working with the word processor. Include instructions for how to change fonts and how to format and use header, footer, and heading settings.)

<h2>Step 1.

Open your word processor to a blank document. Name the document "Last Name_Project # Document setup_Class_Semester Year" and save it somewhere you can easily find it again.

<h2>Step 2.

Set your font to **(*Instructor insert: your desired font)**, and set your font size to **(*Instructor insert: your desired font size)**.

<h2>Step 3.

Go into the headings settings and create heading formatting for three levels (Heading 1, Heading 2, and Heading 3) and the title.

<h2>Step 4.

Add page numbers **(*Instructor insert: Input other header or footer type information for the style guide you have your students working in)**.

(*Instructor suggestion: These steps should be adapted either to the style guide you're assigning or to be more flexible for students if they're designing their own style guide.)

>

<h2>Submit and Reflect

Prepare to submit your document with page numbers, your name, and heading settings. Submit your document to the assignment folder and include a reflection that identifies whether you knew how to do these steps already and whether you are unfamiliar with other elements of the document setup.

While setting up the document at the beginning can help with certain aspects of the document design and using the technology to its capacity, consider the processes that students will do toward the end as well. For example, adding end citations is often a last step for writers (ourselves included!), but students may not be aware of the functions of their word processor that allow them to format the hanging indent on their works cited or references page. They also may not be aware of the issues related to autoformatting from within the word processor, so a specific activity that asks students to check their formatting would be useful.

Learning Activity 8.3: Adding Your References

<h1>Intro Header

<h2>Read

(*Instructor insert: Add the style guide information, even if you've already given it to them. Also include how-to videos/documentation for hanging indents in the specific word-processing application students are using).

<h2>Format/Add

Write and format end citations for three of the sources you'll be using in your essay. Remember we're using **(*Instructor insert: Identify required citation style)**, so your sources will need to be formatted according to that style guide. Keep in mind that autoformatting citation tools are frequently incorrect. If you've started with the autoformatting, please make sure you use our class resources to double-check the order of information, punctuation, and other formatting (especially italics and capitalization).

After you've formatted three sources, **(*Instructor suggestion: We're assuming you are using a citation style that uses hanging indents, like APA or MLA. If you're not, you'll want to adapt this section to articulate the remaining requirements for the formatting of the bibliography)**, you'll want to set your references to have hanging indents. To do this, you'll highlight the citations and then set the hanging indents using the special indent features on your word processor. >

<h2>Submit

Submit the document with your three formatted sources with hanging indents to the assignment folder.

Making specific assignments like Learning Activities 8.2 and 8.3 may appear like a bit of overkill; however, the point we are making is that many instructors assume students already know these functions in their word-processing applications. By designing and implementing these assignments, you will know that everyone has equal access to knowledge on how to format their papers. It also gives credit to students for things they're already having to do. Depending on what you're teaching, you might make this a bonus activity so those who need the help can take advantage of it.

Teaching Revision and Polish

Again, in this chapter, we assume that readers have tried-and-true revision activities for revising alphabetic text. We do suggest, however, giving students some choices in those revision activities. Asking students to choose a revision strategy and then to reflect on that choice can help students do more than go through the motions. Providing students with polishing choices also gives them more agency and allows them to meaningfully reflect upon what type of polishing work their project actually needs. In addition to what we typically consider in revising alphabetic text, we have other considerations when teaching with digital technologies. When considering the technology use and online nature of these particular courses, having students check their alphabetic texts for accessibility is important. When documents are created and are intended to live digitally, we want students to be in the habit of checking those elements. Accessibility checking has come a long way, and most programs have a feature that will allow you to check for accessibility. Those features specifically see accessibility as something readable by a screen reader. However, we should have students set up a document in ways we already know are accessible.

An accessibility check activity would either include readings or videos about accessibility or come after you have taught a mini-lesson on accessibility of documents. At a minimum, you'll want to share how students can check for and produce alt text for images (and if you are asking them to produce tables, then tables as well) in the word-processing documents they are using. This type of an activity might ask students to complete some or all of the following:

1. Make sure that all of the headings are formatted within the document settings **(*Instructor note: This should have been completed in Learning Activity 8.2, but you'll want to double-check)**.
2. Make sure you have alt text for any images and that any tables or figures are in plain text or have alt text.
3. Check that links are functional with appropriate permissions set for the visited webpage or artifact.
4. Use a precise language for hyperlinks (don't copy and paste in long URLs, and don't say "follow link here"—instead, provide a descriptive link like "home page" or "synthesis worksheet").
5. Use an accessibility checker.
6. Make sure to write in plain language.

Technology Toolbox: Accessibility Checkers

- WAVE
- Crownpeak
- Built-in checker in Adobe PDF, Microsoft Word, and Google Docs

If you ask students to use an accessibility checker, you will likely need to provide them suggestions for which ones to use. Most students find at least a few things to change; instead of trying to identify what they changed, consider prompting a reflection section of the assignment that discusses changes.

Connecting Ideas

As we believed when we were writing this chapter, we expect you already have a lot of activities you use to help students produce alphabetic text and just need some reminders about how that production changes in an online setting. You can use the chapters in Part 2 to help students read and analyze images, alphabetic text, videos, and audio to prepare for an alphabetic deliverable or for a deliverable that consists of other media. The next few chapters will give you tools to help students take Parts 2 and 3 and produce other modalities, media, and genres.

Websites and Applications

Adobe PDF built-in checker: https://www.adobe.com/accessibility/pdf/pdf-accessibility-overview.html
Crownpeak: https://www.crownpeak.com/
Google Docs built-in checker: https://support.google.com/docs/answer/6282736
Microsoft Word built-in checker: https://support.microsoft.com/en-us/office/improve-accessibility-with-the-accessibility-checker-a16f6de0-2f39-4a2b-8bd8-5ad801426c7f
Teach Access: https://teachaccess.org/
W3: https://www.w3.org/WAI/tutorials/tables/caption-summary/
WAVE: https://wave.webaim.org/

9

Static Visual Texts

"Static visual texts" is a vague, encompassing term on purpose. Any image or visual text that isn't dynamic (i.e., includes movement or other media, like videos and animated gifs . . . you know, like the magical moving photographs from the Harry Potter universe) counts, which can be a wide variety of digital and physical pieces. You might consider prompting students to think about how their piece can or needs to be used in both digital and physical spaces and the affordances and constraints that come from the shift. For example, restaurant menus are common visual texts that live both digitally and physically, and infographics live in digital spaces and many can be printed. Considering these nuances will be an important part of both you assigning and students completing a static visual text.

A static visual text is a text that relies very heavily on its visual components to convey its message. But that doesn't mean the text is void of any alphabet elements; it means that the alphabetic elements can't stand on their own and be effective. Our guidelines of social presence, time and social justice, and accessibility suggest that when we teach the productions of static visual texts, we need to make sure we're helping students understand the interplay between images and text as well as providing time and space for students to explore these connections. You also need to be sure students are exploring accessibility of their work and be aware of design features that can assist them in making their work accessible and effective in specific rhetorical contexts.

Designing the Instructions

When designing the instructions for a static visual image assignment, just as with assigning other types of texts, you'll want to select the purpose for your students. They'll have already done the reading and analysis of the content, but your instructions will need to articulate what they should do with that content. Will they make an argument? Provide information? You'll also want to decide whether you're going to have students create a single image like an Instagram post, create a static text that has multiple images like an infographic, create a series of images for a professional brand or a collection, or create something else. You might envision a project that relies on static images in a variety of ways, or you might allow students to do that envisioning themselves.

Additionally, in the section of your instructions where you are articulating the parameters of the assignment, you'll want to be sure you explain:

1. Will you be establishing the type of static text? Will students be selecting? For example, will you be assigning an infographic? A poster? A social media post? Letting students pick?
2. How many texts will students be creating? For whom? For example, if you're asking students to create infographics, you might have them create two for two different audiences.
3. Will this text be intended to live digitally, in print, or both? If both, how might the text need to change? Will students be making that decision? For example, students might create menus or brochures that both live in physical and digital spaces but look and feel different in those spaces because of affordances and constraints.

Major Assignment Excerpt 9.1 articulates the answers to these questions. The running example in this chapter is an infographic, as it requires the finding and editing of static images and requires a balance of alphabetic text and images in a way they work together.

Major Project Excerpt 9.1: Project Parameters for Static Images (Infographic)

<h2>Project Parameters

For this project, you will be creating **two** infographics that provide information on the genres you've been analyzing. You will need to select **two** different **audiences** for your infographics. The **purpose** of your infographics is to give this audience information on the discourse of your chosen professional community in a clear, concise, professional, and engaging format. These infographics are intended to live digitally.

<h2>Articulating Audiences

One audience should be individuals who are new to this professional community. They could be undergraduate or graduate students, new graduates, people new to the profession, or those who are changing careers.

>

The other audience should be a more general audience. This could be friends or family, the general public, etc. For example, what kinds of discourse—communication, language, writing, etc.—do mechanical engineers use in their profession? What about surgery nurses or anthropologists? What style of writing do these genres utilize?

If part of your goal is to have students working in a specific technology, then you'll want to articulate that to them in the instructions; otherwise, you'll just want to provide students with an activity that prompts them to select a technology. When you craft prompts that ask students to select their own technology (or ones that address more than one purpose or audience like the example above), we recommend asking students to submit a proposal. You might make this part of the instructions for the major assignment or build it as a scaffolding assignment and then ask your students to include responses to some of the questions in the excerpt in Major Project Excerpt 9.1.

When establishing grading criteria, you'll want to make sure you're assessing students on accessibility (the Major Project Excerpt 10.2 has an example of this for video; for static images, at a minimum, you'll want alt text and consideration for color blindness). Your grading criteria for static images should also include layout and design of the image being required.

Major Project Excerpt 9.2: Static Image-Specific Grading Criteria

<h2>Grading Criteria: **(*Instructor note: Criteria are specific to infographics; you may also use criteria listed in Chapters 8, 10, and 11.)**

- Includes alt text for every image
- Includes image credits for every image you didn't create
- Uses white space to improve readability
- Uses placement/parallelism for flow and readability
- Uses different font formats in different heading levels (for example, Heading 1 and Heading 2 are different)
- Uses the same font format for the same heading levels (for example, Heading 1 is the same font throughout)
- Headings, headers, and footers are formatted for accessibility
- Submitted as a link or **(*Instructor insert: articulate what file type like .png, jpeg, PDF)** file type

After you've designed your instructions, you'll want to design the scaffolding steps that students will need to take to create their static image.

Scaffolding

Scaffolding assignments for static visual text production often center on finding/collecting images (be sure to revisit Chapter 4 regarding copyright), but they also need to have students practice changing small elements of the pieces to learn the tools of the application they're using. In our extended example in this chapter, all students are creating an infographic using the same program (that the instructor would assign). We've included notes for what to change if you've elected to have students select their own technology.

Teaching the Conventions

The conventions of static images depend upon the purpose of the image. Even within the same delivery method (say, infographics), the purpose of the infographic will alter the choices students make. For example, if the infographic is intended to provide information, students might include more alphabetic text, but if it's designed to be persuasive, then they might use more images to engage audience emotions. The delivery method, though, will also impact the conventions. Infographics are expected to have both words and images/figures/tables and be formal in nature. In contrast, memes are not intended to be formal, and they play on the audience understanding the particular brand of humor being conveyed.

When assigning a static visual text, we suggest you start with an activity in which students analyze static visual texts, focusing on the ways words and images work together to send a message. You can have a more general, even fun, assignment in which you have students analyze memes or magazine covers. We also highly suggest you have them analyze the particular genre of the static visual text you are assigning. You'll find an example to help with the analysis of a specific genre that you can adapt in Chapter 8, Learning Activity 8.1. These types of activities are necessary to help students understand what elements are concrete and flexible in the creation of specific types of genres. After students understand what's expected from the content of their assignment or what the rhetorical situation of the image requires, you'll still want to have students consider conventions of the static visual genre they are producing.

Teaching Preproduction

Before students start putting together their static visual texts, they'll need to plan what they want to do and then prep their materials. For planning, you'll want students to sketch out their plan for the layout, design elements, and collecting and preparing their images. Students' plans for layout and design might happen on paper (they might sketch a layout and list potential fonts and colors), or it might happen directly in the program they're using to create the text. Part of the collection and preparation should or could include:

- figuring out what images they want or need (you might prompt them to distinguish between wanting and needing);
- finding images, such as those that are
    - borrowed (downloaded or a screenshot of an image),
    - student generated (screenshots, creative graphics, taken photos, etc.), and
    - checked for ethical use (revisit Chapter 4 for activities on teaching ethics and thinking about permissions of both borrowed and student-generated images);
- cropping;
- shading and using filters;
- resizing;
- changing the colors of an image to match their color scheme; and
- making an image transparent.

> ***AI-Generated Images***
>
> Once you prompt students to find or make images for a project, they might use generative AI applications to help with both finding or producing images. Prompting students to use AI image-generation and editing applications might help radically decrease any anxiety they have about not being artistically inclined. This prompting, however, requires that you have a discussion with students about the affordances, constraints, and ethics of using AI. Don't scare them, but open up the conversation and walk through an example comparing AI- and human-generated images before setting them loose to generate at will.

The upcoming "Teaching the Technologies" section has more on helping students become familiar with a technology, but Learning Activity 9.1 hones in on the idea that students need guidance for what to focus on. The assignment doesn't, however, have the secondary goal to click around and figure out how to do a few small things. This particular assignment has students use what's already on their operating systems, but the "Teaching the Technologies" section highlights programs specifically intended for more robust image manipulation. How students are preparing images depends largely on what technology they're using and how much time you have built into the course for learning technologies. If students are using a program like Adobe Photoshop, which has a relatively steep learning curve, then students will need more time and guidance in figuring out the tools, whereas a fun assignment prompting students to play with a profile picture is probably enough to teach formatting functions in easier applications like Adobe Express and Canva.

Learning Activity 9.1: Taking and Preparing a Screenshot

<h1>Intro Header

<h2>Read

Identify the operating system on your computer. Read the support materials for taking screenshots and adjusting images hyperlinked below: **(*Instructor insert: You'll want to hunt down the support pages for each of these operating systems for taking and adjusting screenshots.)**

- MacOS
- Windows
- Chromebook
- Linux

If you plan to use your phone for this work, you'll need to search for "how to take a screenshot" for your particular phone. If you have trouble finding help, please let me know.

<h2>Collect and Adjust

1. Using the support materials provided, take a screenshot of something you plan to use in your project.
2. Open your screenshot, click "Save As," and name the file "LastName_ScreenshotPractice_Original_Date".
3. Resize the image to 1200px width **(*Instructor insert: You'll want to include instructions for resizing depending on the program)**.
4. Crop the image to the visual you want to see within the frame.
5. Save your file as "LastName_ScreenshotPractice_NewImageName_Date".

>

6. Go to our class Slides.
    - Find the slide with your name on it (they're in alphabetical order by last name).
    - Upload your original screenshot image to your slide.
    - Upload your adjusted screenshot image to your slide.
    - List the steps you took to find the image, discuss why you selected this image and why you cropped to this particular visual, and then reflect on how the process went (What was easy? Fun? How did you overcome any difficulties?).

(*Instructor insert: You'll want to link to a Google Presentation that you've made for the class. You'll need to make a frame for each student and put their name on it.)

<h2>Comment

Using the comment feature of Google Slides, leave one comment for two classmates (leave a comment for someone who doesn't have a comment yet). Your comment should either focus on the image (Was it blurry? Was it big enough?) or their experience with finding and editing the image (Did you run into similar issues? Was your process the same?).

After students find and prepare the images, they'll also want to consider how they're going to cite those images and the alt text they need to use. For example, you could revise Learning Activity 9.2 to prompt students to draft alt text language and then review one another's drafts. In some cases, like infographics, students will be using images within a design space to create a complex static text. In that case, students will need to think about citations and alt text for all of the pieces they include. In other cases, students may be using just a single image, so they'll need to think about citations and alt text for just that one image (or maybe for alphabetic text on that image).

Learning Activity 9.2: Sketching the Infographic

<h1>Intro Header

<h2>Read

(*Instructor insert: Select articles about specific topics such as designing for accessibility, creating layouts, using visuals, emphasizing important information, creating graphics, etc.)

>

<h2>*Layout*

Plan the layout of your infographic. You can hand-sketch the layout of where the text and images will be (***Instructor insert: examples of infographics**). Then, snap a photo and upload. If you'd rather start building in Venngage, the program we're using for these infographics, you can do that and just include placeholders for content (like "I'll say great stuff here"). As you're planning your infographic, consider the importance of design. Remember to keep accessibility in mind as you're planning.

If you're planning to start your sketch directly in Venngage, please do the following:

1. **(*Instructor insert: Decide if you're going to have students select a template or create from scratch. An affordance of the template is it takes some of the design pressure off of students, but it can often be restrictive. An affordance of the empty infographic is that students have control over the layout and design. You'll want to select which direction students should go and identify that here in step one.)**
2. Make sure you know how to share with the class:
   a. Click the Share button in Venngage.
   b. At the bottom of the box that pops up, you'll see "Share a link to," and you'll want to make sure it says "to view." **(*Instructor suggestion: Ensure the language you use in these steps are the same in the specific application you assign the students.)**
   c. Then, copy and paste the link into the discussion board when prompted in the instructions below.

<h2>*Design*

Plan the design aspects of your infographic. What color schemes, font type and size, etc., do you plan to use? This can be done by either showing in Venngage or by telling through creating a bullet list of design issues you are addressing.

<h2>*Submit*

Your submission should include the layout and design for each infographic. If they are not text-based, simply link to your layout and design pieces. If you include links, make sure you have a document in your Google Drive folder that contains those links as well. Also include a reflection on the following:

>

- **Technologies**
    - **Previous experience:** What previous experience do you have with this type of multimodal production? Which technologies have you used during these experiences?
    - **Technology/application**: How do you feel about using Venngage? Where do you plan to go for help with the program?
- **Considerations**
    - What excites you about this multimedia project? Why?
    - How might you use what you learn for future academic or professional projects?
    - What are you concerned or worried about? Why?

Teaching the Technologies

Just like any other technology, be sure you give students time and space to learn how the technology works.

> ***Technology Tip: Assigning Professional Applications***
>
> Professional graphic artists who produce infographics use applications like Adobe InDesign to produce their work. And whereas professional applications like Adobe InDesign and Photoshop give users precise control over their project, the learning curve for such applications is steep. Many applications marketed to educators, like Canva and Adobe Express, are both easier to learn and provide templates students can initially adopt for their project and then adapt as they continue to design and develop. We're not suggesting you don't assign something like InDesign; we're just cautioning you that the more complex the application, the more time you need to dedicate to low-stakes activities in which students learn the technology.

Learning Activity 9.2 starts to do some of that for Venngage by having students do low-stakes work that gets them in the program and clicking on things, but this activity assumes you're going to be selecting the technology for your students. Learning Activity 9.2 could also be broken into two activities: one that requires a hand-drawn sketch and one that has students move that sketch into the program. If you're allowing students to select their own technology, that will look different than if you're asking students to all use the same technology.

In either case, you can ask students to do a particular set of the same activities (insert photo, add shading and highlighting, etc.); however, if students are using self-selected technologies, then you need to build in more time because they'll be responsible for finding their own support resources like Learning Activity 9.3.

Learning Activity 9.3: Drafting the Infographic—Finding and Using Help

<h1>Intro Header

<h2>Select

Identify the application you plan to use for the infographic. Think about your experience with this particular tool. Answer one of these two questions:

- If using an application that's new to you, how do you plan to learn it?
- If this is not a new tool for you, then how much do you know about it? How will you prompt yourself to learn something new in the application?

<h2>Search

To complete this activity, you might go to the website for the application you've selected, go straight to YouTube, do a generic web search, etc. You'll want to search for how to do the following and then select a resource for each element:

- Upload an image
- Change images within the program
- Add text
- Change font style/color

Collect the URLs for each help video/article you find.

<h2>Submit and Reflect

In this discussion board, post the URLs (at least one for each search above) and a reflection that discusses what else you might need help with when you start using this application.

Teaching Revision and Polish

When asking students to polish their static visual texts, you'll want to be sure they're focusing on bigger picture elements like texts and images working together and various aspects of layout and design, as well as the smaller elements of image cropping, color contrast, word choice, citations, etc. Regardless of which aspect you have students focus on, ask them to do a *before* and *after* image with a reflection. This is an important part of the revision process for static visual texts because even the smallest change can make a big difference, and sometimes, students need to see a side-by-side to understand what those differences are. The before and after images allow students to focus on the impact of their piece both as a whole and as discrete parts.

> *Learning Activity 9.4: Revising Your Infographic*
>
> **<h1>Intro Header**
>
> ***<h2>Before You Revise***
>
> 1. **(*Instructor insert: Include readings about layout and design. Based on the readings you have access to, you might want to alter the layout and design elements listed below).**
> 2. Take a screenshot of your draft before making changes, create a new word-processing document, and paste the image into that document. This document should be titled "LASTNAME_RevisingInfographics_DATE." **(*Instructor insert: If you're using a particular space, like Google Workspace, then prompt students to create a document particular to that space.)**
>
> ***<h2>Revise***
>
> 1. Go into your drafts and revise any three of the following layout and design elements:
>   - proximity, alignment, repetition, and contrast
>   - chunking, queuing, and filtering
>   - page layout and columns
>   - typography
>   - titles and headings
> 2. After you make changes, either take another screenshot and upload to your Revising Infographics document, or add the link to your revised project in that document.
> 3. In the document, write a reflection that discusses the types of changes you made and how/why those changes improved the project.
>
> ***<h2>Submit***
>
> Submit your Revising Infographics document to the assignment folder.

Students need to be aware of the impact that color choices (and contrasts) can have on a color-blind or color-sensitive viewer; they similarly need to be aware of the impact an overly crowded/busy design might have on someone who is ADHD, anxious, or neurodivergent. When designing an assignment for checking for accessibility, you might prompt students to check for:

- color choices accounting for color-blind individuals;
- appropriate alt text for images, tables, figures (and other non-text elements) to aid screen readers;
- use of formatted headings to aid navigation with a screen reader;
- exclusion of culturally specific information (unless it's intended for a specific cultural audience); and
- accessible language use.

Technology Tip: Accessibility Resources

Provide students with resources for how to do these accessibility checks and why. For example, you might want to direct students to things like Adobe's blog post, "Why is color accessibility important?" (Gupta, 2021), W3's (2017) "Tips and Tricks," or other resources and examples on accessible language from places like Pudding and the US government.

Connecting Ideas

The work students completed in Part 2 can help them do the work of this chapter. In this chapter, we don't provide graphic design instruction, but we do provide small steps to getting students to use images in conjunction with text in order to make meaning. Regardless of modality, helping students articulate how the media work together for their audience is important. We can't have alphabetic text without document design (that is both visual and accessible to the blind), and we can't have images that are accessible without alphabetic text. This work becomes particularly tricky when trying to teach these concepts across distances. The work done in this chapter can also be built upon and help support the work of Chapters 10 and 11 by providing space for students to start working with visuals and text to create a variety of multimedia deliverables.

Websites and Applications

Adobe Express: https://www.adobe.com/express/
Adobe InDesign: https://www.adobe.com/products/indesign.html
Adobe Photoshop: https://www.adobe.com/products/photoshop.html
Canva: https://www.canva.com/
Google Slides: https://docs.google.com/presentation/
Venngage: https://venngage.com/
Nielsen Norman Group: https://www.nngroup.com/articles/designing-effective-infographics/
Plain Language (government site): https://www.plainlanguage.gov/
The Pudding (accessible language example): https://pudding.cool/2022/02/plain/?fbclid

10

Video and Audio

Video and audio production are critical twenty-first-century digital literacies. Since they have become more affordable and easier to produce and distribute, *younger* folks are expected to have audio and video production skills. When applying our guidelines of social presence, time and social justice, and accessibility to the teaching of video production, we need to be sure we're assigning activities that don't assume what students know or have had access to, and we should provide them with the time and space to learn both the processes and the technologies, especially when we're not in a classroom together.

In this chapter, our example activities focus on video that doesn't involve going out and recording a variety of different shots. Based on the prep work we've suggested so far, you might be more likely to have students either recording themselves or using a compilation of images/slides/other visuals. If you see this as a project where you'll be asking students to go out into the world and record their own video footage, then you'll need more support. Try visiting other faculty with more experience assigning video production (like art or journalism instructors) or web resources like the Adobe Education Exchange.

Although we focus on video in this chapter, we suggest that most audio projects require the same or very similar activities. For example, students can record both audio and video from a variety of devices many of them already own. Most audio- and video-editing applications provide layers or tracks so students can incorporate multiple assets (materials they recorded along with audio or video texts they found) into the production. Both audio and video projects require more processing power, hard-drive space, and specific guidelines for exporting and publishing.

Because students don't want to rerecord elements if they don't have to, the activities and suggestions in this chapter are all activities to help students prepare to create the video or audio production. That's not to say editing can't or won't happen; however, with activities that encourage prep work, students will have less stress in the postproduction process. The application you select can also determine the level of preparation students will need. Programs that allow for easier editing tend to have steeper learning curves, but they allow for changes to be made more easily after production starts. Easier-to-use applications give less control over editing. These are the types of variables to keep in mind as you're deciding on applications when designing your assignment. Especially if you are new to teaching audio or video production, be kind to yourself as you figure out all the variables. As with many first-time assignments, consider inviting students to help during the process and to provide feedback afterward so you can revise the assignment before you next teach it.

Much of what we suggest in the following sections is useful when teaching video and audio in an in-person classroom as well. What makes this more difficult online is the lack of looking-over-their-shoulder workshop time, the issues of access when students aren't on or near a campus, and the inability to quick-correct when students aren't quite meeting the goals of the project. For these reasons, the scaffolding of the project is critical to student success because it serves in helping you to see red flags before students waste too much time.

Designing the Instructions

Before assigning a video assignment, like any other production activity, the purpose of the video needs to be clear as the purpose will guide the parameters you give for that video. Is this a reflection video? A video recording of a presentation? Is it informative? Persuasive? TEDx style? Ignite style? A digital poster? The answer will determine the guidelines you give to your students about length, tone, their inclusion of static images or slides, if a talking head is necessary, or if they need to shoot their own video.

After you've established the purpose, you can start articulating your instructions. Much of the content is likely to come from the reading, analysis, and synthesis activities suggested in Part 2. In other words, before making the video—probably even before planning the video—students will need to have already done the information gathering. They'll need to have done analysis and synthesis of what they found or were provided, and the instructions for the video activity will need to articulate how they're going to use what they've done so far to produce this video.

While writing the instructions, you'll also want to outline your expectations for technology. In some cases, you'll want to recommend a specific video production tool (if your institution has access), but at other times, you'll want to let students select a tool with which they're already comfortable. This decision should largely be based on how much time students have to produce the video and how steep the learning curve is on the tool. For example, Adobe Premiere

Pro, like many premium Adobe products, has a steep learning curve—it takes a while to master simple tasks, but in turn it gives you a lot of control. If students have three weeks to create the video, you may want to stay away from difficult programs like Premiere Pro as there won't be enough time to scaffold. In comparison, Adobe Premiere Rush better balances learnability and editing, and it has a robust mobile application and interface; however, it is still complex enough to need time to learn. The video editing tools in Adobe Express or Canva have almost flat learning curves but do not allow for much in terms of design or editing. Ease of use is one way to be accessible, but you'll want to explore the accessibility resources for any technology you prescribe and consider letting students select ones they're familiar with. Be warned, however: you may have a few students who have been shooting and editing video for a long time. Many times, these experienced students ask to use more advanced video-editing software, so we recommend having a "or other video-editing software you propose" option to accommodate those students.

The example Major Project Excerpt (10.1) technology selection will help guide how students submit their work as drafts and for the final version of their video or audio text. The online submission of a video is complicated. In an in-person class, you can have a session where students bring their videos to class and view them. If you're prescribing a production technology, then you'll want to clearly articulate how students should submit for feedback and grading. If you're allowing students to select their technology, then you'll want to give a few options for how to submit their project, as this may depend on the type of program students are using for production. For example, if they're using a web-based program, they can often just send the link. If they're recording to their devices, you'll want to articulate how and where to upload (e.g., YouTube, Google Drive, OneDrive) so they can easily share a link with you and their classmates. This will mean articulating the options students have and instructing them to figure out which submission method they'll need to use.

Major Project Excerpt 10.1: Video Production Technologies

<h2>Technologies

In this project, you'll be selecting your own video production tool. You may want to consider some of the technologies on this list or select one you're comfortable with. As you're selecting your tool, please review the full project prompt and then answer the following questions (you'll be required to submit responses in your proposal):

>

- What video production technology are you using?
- What prior experience do you have with this technology?
- How are you going to access this application?
- Where are you going to find help/support for this application (be specific; provide names of individuals and links to support websites or videos)?

(*Instructor suggestion: When considering technologies and guiding students to consider them, identify the level of editing students will need for the type of video and involvement of video in the project.)

When considering guidelines and assessments for video and audio productions, you'll want to take into account student access—particularly what kind of tools to which students might have access. The video-editing application is just one of many technologies to which students need access when producing a video. They also need hardware and software that helps them record video and audio; to find and save secondary images, audio, and video clips; and to have access to video publication and distribution outlets. For example, students might be more likely to be able to record audio for their video on their phone, or they might only be able to rely on their laptop microphone to record the audio for their video. This question of tools can impact the production quality, and so considering what tools students have access to is an important part of outlining the requirements for the video. Raw video footage takes up a lot of space, and robust video-editing programs can take a lot of working memory. If students have older machines, they might not be able to use certain applications. In college classes, we've sometimes suggested students use external hard drives when producing larger video assignments.

Group Projects to Support Production Accessibility

Producing audio or video projects requires access to, and the knowledge to use, complicated hardware and software. Even if all your students own mobile devices, not all are likely to have the same capabilities for audio or video recording. Even more simplistic audio- and video-editing software still requires time and energy to learn to use. One way to balance and distribute the accessibility needs of all the students in the class is to assign groups to produce audio or video projects. Before the project assignment, create a survey asking students about their previous experience with production equipment and software, their access to specific pieces of hardware (detailing

>

the specifications) and software, as well as what they desire to learn about the production, editing, and distribution process. You can then use the results of the survey to group students in such a way that balances access, previous experience, and knowledge with learning goals.

You also need to teach students about product accessibility. How are they going to make their videos and audio recordings accessible for a diverse audience? Students will need to learn about captioning for video and transcriptions for audio. Thinking beyond disability: how are they going to be culturally or linguistically accessible (e.g., not using jargon)? Whether the video or audio deliverable is accessible can become a grading criteria. Remember, it's okay to start small—the first time you assign an audio or video project, just focus on transcripts or captioning. The next time, incorporate a step that engages cultural awareness.

Major Project Excerpt 10.2: Project Accessibility

<h2>Project Accessibility

You will need to make sure that your video is accessible. Specifically, you need to make sure that your video is captioned (automatically; even if you use speech to text, go in and edit the captions so that they accurately represent what is being said). You'll also want to make sure your project is linguistically accessible (don't use jargon your intended audience won't know). If you speak in the video, be sure your speech is not too fast (consider testing it with a few people). Finally, make sure your project is viewable/visible by those for whom it is intended (check your settings to make sure it's restricted to and open to your intended audience).

The grading criteria should also include elements like video or audio length, points that need to be covered in the clip in order to serve its purpose, and video or audio quality. Video or audio quality in grading criteria should heavily depend on whether or not students have a space in the classroom (or on campus) to rent or use professional-quality recording equipment. Teaching video online frequently means students won't have access to tools and technologies, even if they live near or on campus. If they don't, then the quality of the video or audio itself should *not* be part of the grading criteria. However, things like speed of speaking voice can be added, as this is something within the students' control. You can easily adapt Major Project Expert 10.3 for an audio assignment like a podcast.

Major Project Excerpt 10.3: Video-Specific Grading Criteria

<h2>Grading Criteria

(*Instructor note: These criteria are specific to video. You may also use criteria listed in Chapter 8, 9, and 11.)

- Video is **(*Instructor insert: required time length.)**
- Video includes correct captions **(*Instructor insert: If assigning audio only, like a podcast, include transcription here instead of captions.)**
- Video URL functions and can be accessed by instructor and classmates
- Background audio plays at an appropriate level that does not overpower the speaker
- All images and borrowed clips are given credit **(*Instructor insert: If assigning audio only, like a podcast, change this to audio clips or background music.)**

Again, we emphasize observable tasks that are equally weighted to provide time and space choices to students. After you've designed the prompt and grading criteria, design the steps you'll have students take to complete the video or audio recording.

Scaffolding

Scaffolding assignments are necessary for any production activity but are particularly important for video and audio production. We can't assume that students are adept at creating them just because they are familiar with watching videos or listening to podcasts. In video production, having students sketch their plans, create materials to be used in the video, script for the video or audio text, and think about how to polish and revise these types of texts, are all elements that need attention. While many of these scaffolding activities should be done before the students start their drafts, they are building blocks that can also be done simultaneously.

Teaching the Conventions

Throughout this book, we've used conventions to mean audience expectations, and for video and audio production, those expectations will vary depending on the purpose and context of the video; just as with alphabetic texts, audio and video texts have multiple genres with a variety of format and content expectations. For example, Ignite-style videos have very strict conventions (five-minute video with twenty slides, giving students fifteen seconds per slide to talk), but if they are creating reflective videos, those parameters might instead be defined by you and by reflection in general.

These types of activities are not uncommon in other forms of production. We have activities for analyzing samples before many new types of projects. This type of activity, like Learning Activity 8.1, can be adapted for video and audio. Once students understand the conventions of the purpose of their video or audio piece, they'll need to learn the conventions or expectations of the delivery method. For example, let's stick with the example of reflective videos. After analyzing videos that focus on the content, length, and other genre features of reflective videos, students will need to learn about timing, audio and video quality, and how audio and images should work together to make their point.

We think it is critical for both you and your students to be prepared for the difference between the results of high-quality video production and post-production and videos made with nonprofessional equipment and applications by people with less experience. Not only do we suggest prompting students to analyze the genre of the video text, we also suggest having them reflect on or have a class discussion about the expectations when you watch a video that's not produced in Hollywood. What sort of elements would make you turn a video off or keep watching? What elements do you expect? You might also have them do a web search for "best practices in creating a video." (You might prompt them with alternative phrasing like "best way" or "what to remember when creating great videos.")

Teaching Preproduction

Preproduction activities ask students to take the information-generating work they've done (the finding, the reading, the analyzing, and the synthesizing from Part 2 and even from Chapters 8 and 9 of this book) and start pulling it together in a way that will help them create the video or audio. For video, preproduction activities should have students using storyboards, collecting images to include in their video, writing scripts, finding sound clips, etc. Audio preproduction might have students planning out their audio clip with an outline, writing a script, finding background music, etc. First, just as with static images, you need to decide if you plan to have students all use the same production and editing applications or if you are comfortable having students select their own applications.

Having students plan that bridge between the synthesis of the information they want to include and the design of the video before starting to collect additional materials for that video (so they know what they want and need to collect) is important. One way of doing this is by having students use storyboards to plan out each scene in their video. Storyboarding can be a useful step because it can help students plan out the timeline of the story they want to tell with their video regardless of the purpose of that video, and it gives them space to identify the needs based on how they want the video to play out. In Learning Activity 10.1, we provide scaffolding for creating a storyboard for a video, but these instructions could be adapted for an audio production as well.

Learning Activity 10.1: Creating a Storyboard

<h1>Intro Header

<h2>Read

- Spend 60 minutes reading your content synthesis activity from **(*Instructor insert: name/date/location of the last synthesis activity students completed)**.
- Spend 30 minutes reading **(*Instructor insert: 1–2 readings about how storyboards translate to videos)**.

<h2>Complete Your Storyboard

For this activity, you can either do a digital storyboard (using Google Slides, PowerPoint, or boxes in a word processor) or you can download, print, and complete a paper storyboard **(*Instructor insert: Add one or two storyboard templates to be printed; plenty are available online)**. In either case, you'll want to plan out your video. In your slides, you'll identify what you want to put in each frame of the video with any text, voiceover, or effects listed in the speaker notes. In each box, draw what each frame of the video will look like with the voiceover, effects, editing transition, etc., listed on the lines below. You should have at least eight frames completed (that doesn't mean you'll *only* have eight frames for your video, but you need to be at least that far in the process).

(*Instructor note: Storyboarding is an activity that can be a very simple planning activity, as done here, but some storyboarding applications get more into the craft of designing videos and often have steeper learning curves and higher prices. These are programs like Adobe XD, Storyboarder, etc.)

>

<h2>*Submit and Reflect*

Submit your storyboard and reflection (questions are listed below). If you have completed a digital storyboard, submit the link to your storyboard. If you have completed a paper storyboard, please take a photo of your storyboard and upload it to **(*Instructor insert: indicate where students should place the photo)** then grab the link to your photo and submit it.

<h2>*Reflection Questions*

- How do you feel about your storyboard plan?
- Do you think you can create a video using your storyboard? Why?
- What is your next step in taking your video from sketch to reality?

After students have planned how their video might progress and what each video scene or slide will contain, they'll want to go collect equipment and raw materials. The students' plans for their videos should guide the finding of raw materials, as should the considerations of the ethics of finding texts to use as raw materials such as audio clips, music, and images. (For how to find and manage those texts, see activities in Chapter 4.) You might also, or instead, have students create some of these raw materials (see Chapter 9), but consider how much experience students have, how much time you have allotted for the project, and whether students have access to the equipment necessary. Student access to hardware and software will drive the finding of equipment.

When asking students to collect particular materials and equipment for their video production, consider what tools you are asking students to edit with (Are you prescribing them or letting students pick?). This is important as it will not only determine what students can include and what features are available with the program, but also because the technology determines the equipment needed. If a tool will require equipment students don't have access to or it's unethical to expect access, then you'll want to consider a different tool. Learning Activity 10.2 is a scaffolding step intended to make sure students have all the elements you're requiring of them.

Learning Activity 10.2: Prepping Materials and Equipment

<h1>Intro Header

<h2>*List Materials and Equipment*

Think about what you'll need to complete your project:

>

- Do you have access to a microphone? If you're using a microphone on your smartphone, how are you going to transfer it to the space where you're constructing the video? Will you be using a webcam? If so, do you need to find one?
- What application are you using for video production? Do you have access to it? Have you set up an account? Do you know where you find help for using the application?
- Do you know what images, audio clips, etc., you'll need for your video? Have you collected them?
- Where will you keep copies of all your work? What will be your file naming conventions?

As you consider these questions, make a list of the materials and the equipment you'll need to complete your video.

<h2>Locating Materials and Equipment

After you have your list, write down where the materials are or what you need to do to access them. For example, next to the status of your microphone availability, you might have something like this:

- Microphone: need one; located on phone and plan to save to Google Drive to access on laptop.

Complete your whole list in this way. **(*Instructor note: For each item, you might also prompt students to add a list of resources [e.g., people, websites, videos] to which they can refer if they need help with the materials and equipment.)**

<h2>Testing Materials and Equipment

Some of your equipment might need a trial run, especially the microphone, webcam, and application you're using. Test those elements. Next to the items on your list, identify the steps you took in testing. To stick with the microphone example, you might try doing a recording on your phone, sending it to your laptop, listening to the clip, and then trying to upload it into the application you're using to make the video. List those steps under your equipment/materials list and identify whether the steps were successful.

<h2>Submit and Reflect

Submit to the assignment folder: your materials/equipment list that includes where/how you located and how you tested each item along with the success
>

(or not) of each test. With your list, please include a reflection that covers the following:

- Do you feel prepared to start producing your video? Why or why not?
- What else do you need to do to prepare for video production?

Teaching the Technologies

When teaching the technology for video (or audio) production, be sure you're including enough opportunities for students to work with the production and editing technologies. A learn-the-technology assignment might include a small activity that asks students to:

- find three supporting materials about the technology they're going to use;
- record a 30–60 second test video (or audio) clip so they can hear and see how their equipment records their audio and video elements; and
- prompt students to make 2–3 edits to the short clip.

The goal is to get students clicking around and using the tools in the application they're using in a low-stakes activity that removes the pressure and stress of needing to be perfect for a high grade. These trial runs do not need to take place during the module in which you're having students complete a video; you can instead make it part of another assignment earlier in the class so students are familiar before they have to start planning for and creating their videos. For example, we've prompted students to make quick introduction videos of themselves toward the beginning of a course that will later prompt them to produce a video.

When discussing the production and editing technologies, you'll also want to discuss recording equipment. Provide suggestions like using their smartphone or using earbuds instead of the microphone on their laptop so they can get the microphone closer to their mouth and so that sounds like laptop fan noise has less impact on the quality of their audio. The recording aspect of video also comes with the need to discuss storage. Video files are notorious for being large. The storage and transference of video needs to be planned in advance. Remember that your online students will have limited options for submission; they can't bring you a USB. Prompting students to use cloud storage can help.

After students have recorded pieces, you'll want them to practice editing in the technology. Give students a specific number of things to edit (say, three) with specific ideas for how to edit the particular clip you've asked them to produce. For example, you might ask students to produce a short project pitch as a way to practice with the technologies before the higher-stakes full project. Provide them with helpful suggestions as to what they might edit, like:

- add music to the background,
- clip out a certain spot,
- add a transition before or after the clip, or
- adjust the volume of your audio.

This particular activity has students using a small clip to practice, but the go-edit-three-things activity is a good way to help students learn any new production technology. If you or your students select an application that allows for more involved editing, you could create a separate editing assignment that provides space for more complex edits. If students are using applications with limited editing functionality, you might prompt them to reflect on the three changes they would want to make to a lower-stakes assignment.

Teaching Revision and Polish

For those new to audio and video production, revision can seem overwhelming. Students often resist revising video or audio, especially if it involves rerecording something. Prompt students to address certain types of elements they'll need to polish during the planning stage is very important and contributes to polish in postproduction. Students need enough time to get feedback on their video/audio texts to be able to do something with that feedback. For example, creating activities that prompt students, *before they record*, to revise the image placement in their slides or to practice and then revise their storyboard and script are ways to have students polish before recording.

Students may resist scripting, but be sure to emphasize that scripting helps keep them to specific time limits (which is especially important in videos that fall into specific conventions like Ignite or TEDx), and it helps the video be more polished, thereby saving time during the editing process. At a minimum, the video is less likely to have verbal fillers that can be distracting (e.g., "like," "umm," "so") when you require your students to script. You might think it's weird that a scripting activity is being included here, but when it comes to video, planning ahead is necessary to have a polished final product.

Learning Activity 10.3: Scripting

<h1>Intro Header

<h2>Read

- Revisit and review your plans for your video so far (20–30 minutes)
- Spend 20–30 minutes reviewing model scripts **(*Instructor insert: Find some model scripts, ideally ones similar to the genre your students are producing.)**

<h2>Write, Practice, and Time It Out

Return to your storyboard and, using your frames as a guide, write a script for each frame. After you've written a full draft of your script, time yourself reading the script out loud and note the time next to each frame on your storyboard. Edit as you go. You might want to organize your script this way:

- Frame 1: I'll say great stuff here
- Frame 2: This is an awesome point I'll make

<h2>Submit

For your initial post, please submit your storyboard and script, including the time it took to read through each storyboard frame noted next to the text you read.

<h2>Comment

Respond to two classmates, focusing on:

- How natural does the script sound (read it aloud yourself)? Or if the script is an outline of ideas rather than verbatim text, determine if it progresses naturally, if anything seems out of logical order, etc.
- Is the script relevant to what's going on in the visual aspect?

(*Instructor insert: Depending on the topic, you may have other things to add to the focus.)

If you're having students use a robust video tool in which they'll have greater editing capabilities (and therefore, a steeper learning curve), you'll want to prompt your students to revise their videos before submitting. These editing activities will need more nuanced instructions that focus on things like transitions within the video, audio volume and quality, shot composition, and animations. There is a long list of potential areas of video production that you can have students focus on. They can't focus on all of them because you need to teach those areas to students in order to require them. The potential areas will also be determined by the type of work you've asked them to do: Are they going out and video-recording things? Are they creating animations? Are they working with slides? If you're asking students to use a more robust tool, you'll need to dedicate more time to helping students learn the tool and use it effectively. This means giving them time, space, and direct instruction on smaller steps and using specific features of the application.

Finally, regardless of the video-editing tools, if students have an audio component, then they need to caption their videos. There are many auto-captioning tools that will convert speech to text, but they are not perfect. Students will still need to check their captions to be sure they accurately reflect what is being said in the video.

Connecting Ideas

In this chapter, we have built on activities and suggestions presented in Part 2 by suggesting ways to take the finding, analyzing, and synthesizing of content and present it using video or audio. Each time we ask students to use a new tool, we need to create activities that help them learn how to use that tool. There is a fine line between teaching literacy and teaching technology; our goal in online literacy courses is to teach students how to learn a technology—this is a form of literacy that is necessary for digital production. This is especially important in our online courses because the course already relies on technologies in order to be a course in the first place. Multimodal production adds more technology in spaces where you can't be looking over their shoulder to help. So far, we've covered the production of alphabetic text, static images, video, and audio. In the final chapter, we cover ways to remix these elements.

Websites and Applications

Adobe Express: https://www.adobe.com/express/
Adobe Education Exchange: https://edex.adobe.com/
Adobe Premiere Pro: https://www.adobe.com/products/premiere.html
Adobe Premiere Rush: https://www.adobe.com/products/premiere-rush.html
Adobe XD: https://www.adobe.com/products/xd/features.html

Canva: https://www.canva.com/
Google Drive: https://www.google.com/drive/
Google Slides: https://www.google.com/slides/about/
OneDrive: http://onedrive.com
PowerPoint: https://office.live.com/start/powerpoint.aspx
Storyboarder: https://wonderunit.com/software/storyboarder/
YouTube: https://www.youtube.com/

11

E-Portfolios, Websites, and Other Remixes

When asking students to build e-portfolios, websites, or remixes (that is, taking work they've already done and reframing it), we need to guide students through the collection of materials, understanding what these elements look like, how and why they'll transform, and how to thread them together in ways that are rhetorically sound and accessible. One of the easiest ways to do reflective reframing is to have students thinking about how they'll repurpose that work at the same time as they're creating it in the first place. For example, if you know you're going to have your students write an essay that they'll later turn into a poster or a podcast, as they're writing the paper, have them think and write about the changes that the shift will have on their work and how digital technologies will provide affordances and constraints moving forward. The modalities and programs you or your students choose in these types of projects will guide what can and can't be done. Having students consider these shifts early on will help them make informed choices that best suit their purposes or help them figure out creative workarounds. Part of teaching digital literacy is helping students understand how to find workarounds and compromises with the technologies they have access to in order to achieve their goals.

E-portfolios, websites, and remixes give students a space to really explore our themes of social presence, time and social justice, and accessibility because they're less rigid than traditional academic genres. Students often see these types of projects as an opportunity to be more creative and to pull their experiences and interests into their learning in authentic ways. The incorporation of time and social justice, as with all the technologies in this text, are critical when asking students to repurpose previous work, and the process of rethinking previous work also takes time. Finally, ensuring the technologies are accessible and overall teaching accessibility are important in spaces where students are sometimes sharing personal struggles or learning. Privacy becomes more of a concern when putting work on the web, even in situations where you can restrict users, and considering the audience is important when restricting users.

Designing the Instructions

Before designing the instructions for the project, you'll want to map to it. How are you going to use and craft previous projects, activities, and materials from the course to help students generate and think forward to the shift in purpose and context that will come when they take on the new portfolio or remix project? What is the course arc that leads to the remixing of materials? Students will need a clear road map for this (see Figure 11.1). Once you decide how you'll lead students to the project, you'll want to be sure you articulate to students what pieces they'll be collecting or reworking to create the new project. This type of project mapping is a type of backward design, or scaffolding, as we discussed in Chapter 2.

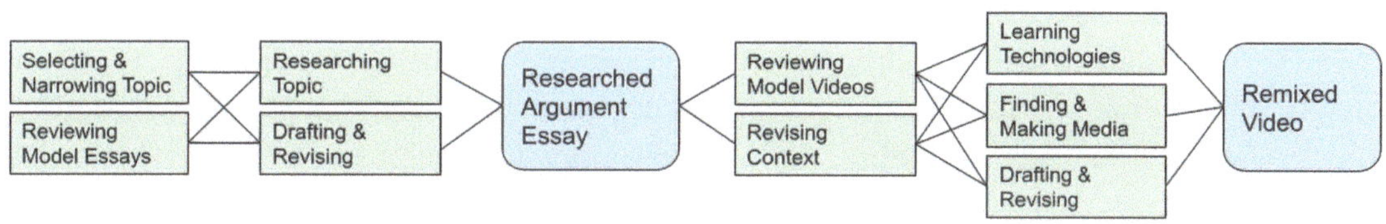

FIGURE 11.1. Simplified Roadmap of Course with a Remix Project

Just as with other production activities, identify the purpose of the project in your assignment instructions; that purpose might be to document learning, to create a website to report on research, or to take an entire project and remix it into a new mode of delivery. Regardless of the purpose or content of the end project, you will want to make it clear to students how to reframe what they have to achieve the new purpose. The instructions should help to make those connections in order for students to re-see the work that they've already done. We have two running examples in this chapter, a learning e-portfolio (from our discussion in upcoming sections) and a remixed video argument (in the upcoming sample activities). A learning e-portfolio is usually an assignment finalized at the end of a course or in larger program of study in which students demonstrate they have met the assigned learning outcomes. Learning e-portfolios typically include multiple examples of student work (both finalized projects as well as homework or in-process materials) and a lot of student reflection on how they learned. A remixed video argument is when an instructor prompts a student to take the research from a traditional alphabetic essay and use it as the base content for an argument developed in another modality (in this case, a video, but it could just as easily be an infographic or an audio file/podcast).

Major Project Excerpt 11.1: Purpose and Context (Remixed Video Argument)

<h2>Purpose and Context

The purpose of this assignment is to use the research and synthesis work you've already completed in this class to make your argument in another media form. The goal is to adapt your argument for a differently articulated audience using the affordances of a different modality. For example, in a video about fire safety, you could use images or clips of lands devastated by wildfire to emotionally charge your audience.

After articulating the purpose of the project and how that purpose will be achieved by working with the content they've already collected and developed, articulate the media and types of technologies students will need to select (ideally, helping them choose in order to best support the purpose and audience). You'll need to clearly articulate the options that students have (both in your class and what digital applications they might use in future) and then break down the assignment requirements based on those options. The options students have will determine the requirements and the grading criteria. For example, for the e-portfolio, you might assign a website or assign a simple folder. For an e-portfolio or a website, a variety of "What You See Is What You Get" (WYSIWYG)-style site builders are available that allow students to start from a template and make the building process happen more smoothly without having the ability to code. However, you'll still want to build in instructions and expectations on design and content, even if students aren't being required to code. For example, you might include mini-lessons on color, contrast, or alignment.

After considering purpose and design, break down requirements and be particular about how those requirements might need to change depending on how much leeway students are given to be creative. For example, in addition to design features, students will need direction on how many website pages to have, the content of those pages, and the organization of those pages. For an e-portfolio website, you might require an "About Me" page, but let students organize the website the way they want. The grading criteria for a learning e-portfolio might include:

- Website includes **(*Instructor insert: Required number of pages)**
- Include pages/sections for **(*Instructor insert: Titles of pages that are required)**

- Page/section ______ should include **(*Instructor insert: Identify the page title, what should be on that page, and a rubric item for each content element.)**
- Each _____ page/section should contain a reflection about what was learned and how you'll apply that learning in the future

Students will need examples of what to look for to ensure their projects are accessible. In Major Project Excerpt 11.2, the grading criteria are specific about options you might require for a video argument; just be clear about the content that must be included.

Major Project Excerpt 11.2: Video Argument-Specific Grading Criteria

<h2>Grading Criteria

(*Instructor note: These criteria are specific to video; you may also use criteria listed in Chapters 8, 9, and 10.)

- Video includes **(*Instructor insert: Required number of transitions)**
- There should be screens/shots for **(*Instructor insert: Titles of screens/shots that are required, e.g., title, section breaks, references)**
- Title screen/shot should include **(*Instructor insert: Identify the page screen/shot, what should be included, and a rubric item for each content element.)**
- Each section should have a specific focus (e.g., history of topic, what others have said/argued about topic, thesis, focused line of reasoning with evidence, conclusion or call to action)
- Video is captioned

After designing your prompt, you'll need to establish checkpoints for students. Many of those checkpoints, especially if students are completing either an e-portfolio or a video (refer to Chapter 10), will take place before students start building, but the technology will also need to be scaffolded just as it was in Chapters 9 and 10.

Scaffolding

Scaffolding for an e-portfolio or a remix should occur throughout the course. This is especially important for learning e-portfolios, as students should be asked to stop and reflect on their learning throughout the class with an eye for the e-portfolio. For a remix, students might also be asked to stop and think about how they might do things differently if they were working in a different modality, or you might ask them to produce invention work in different modalities. For example, when prompting students to develop an argument, have them find images that represent their lines of reasoning or specific evidence. The reflection about how modality impacts meaning can make students more aware of the rhetorical decisions they're making. This will allow students time and space to think critically about the content they'll include in the e-portfolio or remix. Especially in an online asynchronous course, assigning scaffolding and prompt reflection is important, as is explicitly helping students see the connections between the scaffolded assignments, reflections, and the final products.

Teaching the Conventions

Again, project purpose and genre will determine the conventions. When helping students learn about the conventions of the projects they'll be creating, you'll want to start out by having students analyze examples of the specific type of project. If students are creating informative podcasts, you'll want students to analyze and understand the conventions of that particular type of podcast. If they are creating videos that argue a point, you'll want them to view and analyze example videos that do the same (ideally ones that are approximately the same length as the video you are assigning). If students are creating a learning e-portfolio, then you'll want students to analyze learning e-portfolios (especially in contrast to showcase e-portfolios like professional artists produce). Sometimes you'll find you can't always locate the specific type of projects they'll be creating. In that case, you'll want to give examples that are close and have students analyze how they do or don't fit what you're asking them to do. We suggest you find examples for them to analyze rather than having them find the examples, as you understand best what you hope they'll produce. We've designed example analysis assignments that are open-ended, like Learning Activity 8.1, or example analysis assignments specific to the major project where we prompt students to use the final project grading criteria to analyze the examples.

When responding to students in example analysis assignments, be sure you're helping them make the connection between what they're seeing in the samples and what they're required to do. If the podcasts, videos, and e-portfolios are more professional than your students can create in the given time, articulate that to them. If one of the examples makes a move you expect or a move you do not want to see, make sure to tell students about that section (even if it is after they've completed the analysis while you debrief their learning). Help students use the activity to better understand what you're asking them to do. As a way to help manage your time, we recommend you do this in bulk feedback to the class and reach out to individual students who may be completely misunderstanding what they need to do or what the expected conventions are in the final major project.

Teaching Preproduction

Preproduction should begin with the first assignment in the class or the project that will work toward the remix. Students should be made aware of what they're working toward—prompt them along the way to collect materials and reflect on how their purpose changing in the future will impact the work they'll do and decisions they'll make. This archiving or content auditing is critical to do incrementally because, as we remove ourselves from the work we did, remembering the steps we took becomes more difficult.

The timing of assigning reflections or content audits will depend on the level and length of the class. In longer courses that require e-portfolios, you may include stop, collect, and reflect assignments more frequently than in shorter courses. Similarly, when designing courses or units about developing an argument that will be remixed, you might include more activities that prompt students to express ideas and content through images and sound.

While developing an e-portfolio, the initial archive and reflect activity will require students to set up an archival plan and location. Once this is set up, archive and reflect activities can be used anytime during the course. When reflecting on specific assignments, projects, or artifacts, you might ask students to answer the following:

- What are you most proud of? Why?
- What would you continue to work on if you had more time?
- What work did you do to complete this project? I don't want to know what I asked you to do; I want to know what you did (and where you got stuck and overcame your struggles).
- Why did you archive the work you selected? Please be as specific as possible.

To help students connect details from their project to goals and outcomes, we find it useful to remind students to revisit assignment, project, course, and personal goals. You can then ask students to connect what they've learned in the project to the course. You might also ask them to reflect on whether their personal goals have changed.

Especially if the reflections are building toward a web-based e-portfolio, we suggest prompting students to collect artifacts in different media. You might ask them to take pictures or screenshots that represent their process or product. Emotions are also important while reflecting; you might ask students to find images that represent how they felt during the process or after they completed the project. Regardless of how many times you have students run through this archiving and reflecting process, you will need to have students synthesize the reflecting and archiving they've done before they start pulling it together for the e-portfolio. (See Chapter 7 for optional synthesis activities.)

You can also prompt students to think about their research and arguments using modes other than alphabetic texts. Try incorporating some multimedia-to-learn or multimedia-to-reflect assignments to help students develop arguments and to function as remix preproduction activities. These types of activities might include:

- **Identifying and Narrowing a Topic**: Have students use pictures to identify what they want to research versus what they do not want to research, as well as to help identify search terms (see Learning Activity 11.1). They can also use music to reflect upon why they are interested and invested in this topic.
- **Reflecting on Research**: For each secondary source or piece of evidence, prompt students to find a separate image that represents the source/evidence. When they start grouping together sources/evidence to make an argument, can they group the images together as well? Do the images potentially suggest an alternative grouping of sources/evidence? After producing an alphabetic text outline of their argument, students can replace references to sources/evidence with the appropriate images. Do the images prompt them to rethink how they are developing the argument?
- **Introductions and Conclusions**: Prompt students to identify a piece of music that represents why an audience should care about their topic and take the time to read the argument. Ask them to find another piece of music that represents the conclusion of their argument and suggests a call-to-action for the topic.
- **Reviewing the Argument**: Have students record themselves slowly and clearly reading the complete draft of their alphabetic argument. Did reading the argument aloud give them ideas about what changes they

want to make? Prompt them to ask a friend or family member to listen to (not read!) the argument. Where did they stop or replay a section? Where did they make comments? How is their reaction different from the reactions of reviewers who read the draft of the alphabetic argument?

As with any assignment, instructors should prompt students to reflect upon what they learned during the activity and how they will use it to move forward in developing or revising their major project.

Learning Activity 11.1: Using Images to Narrow Your Research Topic

<h1>Intro Header

<h2>Read

Prepare for this exercise by learning about Boolean operators and how they work to improve search results:

(*Instructor insert: Include links to resources about Boolean operators. If you know exactly which search engine you will prompt students to use, you might include instructions for that specific search engine.)

<h2>Prepare

Start a new word-processing document in the shared folder for the course **(*Instructor insert: Provide link to a shared Google or OneDrive folder for the course)**. Title the file "LastName-Visually Explore Research Topic".

<h2>Search

Go to a search engine where you can sort results by modality, specifically image results. Conduct the following searches (be sure to read all of the instructions below before you actually conduct the searches):

1. Key term(s) describing your current topic
2. Based on previous results, key term(s) using the "NOT" Boolean operator
3. Based on previous results, key term(s) using different or more focused key term(s)
4. Based on previous results, key term(s) using the "NOT" Boolean operator

<h2>Reflect

After each search, include the following documentation and reflection material in your shared word-processing document:

>

1. Search term(s) you used
2. Three images that represent the topic you are interested in; briefly describe why they are good representations of what and/or why you are interested
3. One image that does NOT represent the topic you are interested in; briefly describe why, discuss how and why you think that image was part of the results

(*Instructor suggestion: Especially if teaching an asynchronous online course, we suggest instructors provide a demo of this activity. First, students might not know how to easily include the images [e.g., right-click and grab URL of the image's location, download/upload, screenshot]. Second, they might not understand the filtering you expect. One of our favorite examples is to use "caterpillar"; the results will quickly show both the insects as well as the tractors, and you might also get some images from *Alice in Wonderland*.)

<h2>Submit

Copy and paste the URL to your shared word-processing document into the LMS assignment area.

(*Instructor note: Depending on the course timeline, students might benefit from a round of response. It is nice for them to be reminded that not everyone interprets images the same way.)

The rubric for this assignment can be lengthy in terms of the number of searches you require and the amount of information you require students to track. However, we stand by completion rubrics as the best way to consider our theme of time and social justice in our assessment practices. When an activity is going to take a lot of time and require a lot of tasks, students should be given credit for it, and missing a few tasks shouldn't make or break their grade. One way we've helped students manage this work is by developing a worksheet for this type of assignment, which then also helps with the quick assessment of completed work.

If you are giving students space to be more creative, be sure you give them time and space to consider the sections they want to include. If students are creating a website, let them brainstorm what pages they'll need (see Learning Activity 10.1 for an example of planning). If they're remixing an assignment, ask them to complete an activity to consider the elements of the original that should be included in their remix.

Teaching the Technologies

As we have previously noted, e-portfolios don't necessarily have to be websites. Students might produce a digital letter using a word-processing application that can easily incorporate images, tables, and hyperlinks. The digital document allows students to more easily change their design and formatting while also incorporating images and hyperlinks (the "Archiving and Reflecting" activities prepare them with multiple media and example texts to which they might link). However, make sure students know how to copy the links to the pieces they've archived and create a hyperlink in the digital letter document. Demonstrating both of these activities is best shown through screencast videos so students can return to the instructions as needed.

For e-portfolios that are websites, even for WYSIWYG programs, you'll need to give students the opportunity to plan and build in smaller increments in order to practice the technology. Activities that ask students to simply create and share a blank site (so they can practice publishing and sharing the link) is a really useful way to start, especially if you haven't done any other sort of work in the class that requires students to use sites outside of the LMS.

After students have started their sites, you'll want to have them build in small pieces so they can practice and get stuck on the technology. Some ways you can have them do that are to add their selected font and colors to the whole site or to draft individual pages with some content. For e-portfolios, prompt students to build one of their pages. Sometimes starting with their "About Me" page to set up the formatting template for the entire site is easiest. After they have built their the "About Me" page, you might prompt them to reflect with these types of questions:

- Did you run into any problems using the technology? If so, what?
- Was there anything you wanted to do but couldn't figure out how? If so, what?
- Why did you select the font, colors, etc., you did?
- How do you feel about the design of the page? Will you carry it through the rest of the site?

Ideally, you would have students follow up by reviewing one another and providing feedback about format and style.

If you are assigning a remix to video assignment, the two easiest mechanisms to prompt students to learn video technologies is to have them make a low-stakes video, like an introduction to themselves, and to build small pieces of the project at a time. In Chapter 10, we include more detailed ideas on how to teach the technology when using video.

Teaching Revision and Polish

Polishing in e-portfolios, websites, and remixes needs to focus on the alphabetic text, the visual and audio elements, and the ways in which the separate elements work together to create a whole. When asking students to polish their alphabetic text, see examples in Chapter 8. When asking students to focus on the audio or visuals, see Chapter 10. When assigning e-portfolios, we suggest assigning a polishing activity like that associated with the infographic assignment in Chapter 9 (Learning Activity 9.4).

Conclusion: Growing Your Network of Assignments

As with similar books of the applied pedagogy genre, too many good ideas are stuffed in here for you to adapt and adopt in one cycle or iteration of a course. We hope this book sits on your office shelf so you might regularly pull it out when you need a new idea. Or, maybe it is something you grab when a colleague sits and chats with you about what they want to do in their online courses or with their digitally mediated assignments.

Besides sharing this resource with your future self and your colleagues, we hope you'll share how you have adopted, adapted, and developed your own assignments with the larger network of your literacy-learning colleagues at regional and national conferences as well as in pedagogically oriented publication venues. In short, we know our network of assignments has expanded over the years because of our collaboration with one another as well as our sharing and dialoguing with others. We hope you adopt, adapt, and share these activities, as we look to adopt and adapt activities from you.

References

Adam, B. (2004). *Time*. Wiley.

Alem, Y. T. (2019). Critical reflection as motivational strategy of learning critical reading. *Journal of Language Teaching and Research, 10*(4), 683–691. http://dx.doi.org/10.17507/jltr.1004.03

Americans with Disabilities Act of 1990, 42 U.S.C. § 12101 *et. seq*. (1990). https://www.ada.gov/pubs/adastatute08.htm

Anderson, L. W., Krathwohl, D. R., Airasian, P., Cruikshank, K. A., Mayer, R. E., Pintrich, P. R., Raths, J., & Wittrock, M. C. (Eds.). (2000). *A taxonomy for learning, teaching, and assessing: A revision of Bloom's taxonomy of educational objectives* (Abridged ed.). Pearson.

Arbaugh, J. B. (2010). Sage, guide, both, or even more? An examination of instructor activity in online MBA courses. *Computers & Education, 55*(3), 1234–1244. https://doi.org/10.1016/j.compedu.2010.05.020

Arslanova, I., Kotsaris, V., & Tsakiris, M. (2023). Perceived time expands and contracts within each heartbeat. *Current Biology, 33*(7), 1389–1395. https://doi.org/10.1016/j.cub.2023.02.034

AT&T. (2002, July 8). *21st century literacies homepage*. Internet Archive Wayback Machine. Retrieved February 1, 2022, from http://web.archive.org/web/20110716160908/http://www.kn.pacbell.com/wired/21stcent/

Bain, K. (2004). *What the best college teachers do*. Harvard University Press.

Barnes, R. A., & Piland, W. E. (2010). Impact of learning communities in developmental English on community college student retention and persistence. *Journal of College Student Retention: Research, Theory & Practice, 12*(1), 7–24. https://doi.org/10.2190/CS.12.1.b

Bean, J. C. (2011). *Engaging ideas: The professor's guide to integrating writing, critical thinking, and active learning in the classroom*. Jossey-Bass.

Bean, J. P., & Metzner, B. S. (1985). A conceptual model of nontraditional undergraduate student attrition. *Review of Educational Research, 55*(4), 485–540. https://doi.org/10.3102/00346543055004485

Belanoff, P. (2001). Silence: Reflection, literacy, learning, and teaching. *College Composition and Communication, 52*(3), 399–428. https://doi.org/10.2307/358625

Berry, S. (2017). Building community in online doctoral classrooms: Instructor practices that support community. *Online Learning, 21*(2). https://doi.org/10.24059/olj.v21i2.875

Boettcher, J. V., & Conrad, R. (2016). *The online teaching survival guide: Simple and practical pedagogical tips* (2nd ed.). Jossey-Bass.

Boston, W., Diaz, S. R., Gibson, A. M., Ice, P., Richardson, J., & Swan, K. (2009). An exploration of the relationship between indicators of the community of inquiry framework and retention in online programs. *Online Learning, 13*(3), 67–83. http://doi.org/10.24059/olj.v13i3.1657

BYUCopyright. (2017, April 14). *It's a Wonderful Law* [Video]. YouTube. https://youtu.be/0xb3LZK1vcU

Carillo, E. C. (2021). *The hidden inequities in labor-based contract grading*. Utah State University Press.

Cavanagh, S. R. (2016). *The spark of learning: Energizing the college classroom with the science of emotion*. West Virginia University Press.

Center for Applied Special Technology (CAST). (2018). *Universal design for learning guidelines* (Version 2.2). http://udlguidelines.cast.org

Chickering, A., & Gamson, Z. (1987). Seven principles for good practice in undergraduate education. *AAHE Bulletin*, 3–7. https://aahea.org/articles/sevenprinciples1987.htm

Cohn, J. (2021). *Skim, dive, surface: Teaching digital reading*. West Virginia University Press.

Condon, F., & Young, V. A. (Eds.). (2016). *Performing antiracist pedagogy in rhetoric, writing, and communication*. The WAC Clearinghouse; University Press of Colorado. https://doi.org/10.37514/ATD-B.2016.0933

Council of Writing Program Administrators (CWPA). (2008). *WPA outcomes statement for first-year composition*. https://www.in.gov/che/files/WPA_Outcomes_Statement_for_First-Year_Composition.pdf

Dahlstrom, E., de Boor, T., Grunwald, P., & Vockley, M. (2011). *The ECAR national study of undergraduate students and information technology*. EDUCAUSE Center for Applied Research. https://library.educause.edu/resources/2011/10/~/media/files/library/2011/10/ers1103w-pdf.pdf

d'Alessio, M.A., Lundquist, L. L., Schwartz, J. J., Pedone, V., Pavia, J., & Fleck, J. (2019). Social presence enhances student performance in an online geology course but depends on instructor facilitation. *Journal of Geoscience Education, 67*(3), 222–236. https://doi.org/10.1080/10899995.2019.1580179

Darby, F., & Lang, J. M. (2019). *Small teaching online: Applying learning science in online classes*. Jossey-Bass.

Davidson, C. N. (2011). *Now you see it: How technology and brain science will transform schools and business for the 21st century*. Penguin.

Davidson-Shivers, G. V., Rasmussen, K. L., & Lowenthal, P. R. (2018). *Web-based learning: Design, implementation and evaluation* (2nd ed.). Springer.

Dawson, S. (2006). A study of the relationship between student communication interaction and sense of community. *The Internet and Higher Education, 9*(3), 153–162. https://doi.org/10.1016/j.iheduc.2006.06.007

Deil-Amen, R. (2011). *The "traditional" college student: A smaller and smaller minority and its implications for diversity and access institutions* [Conference session]. Mapping Broad-Access Higher Education, Stanford University, CA. https://cepa.stanford.edu/conference-papers/traditional-college-student-smaller-and-smaller-minority-and-its-implications

Dietz-Uhler, B., Fisher, A., & Han, A. (2007). Designing online courses to promote student retention. *Journal of Educational Technology Systems, 36*(1), 105–112. https://doi.org/10.2190/ET.36.1.g

Faden, E. (2007, March 1). *A Fair(y) Use Tale* [Video]. The Center for Internet and Society, Stanford Law School. http://cyberlaw.stanford.edu/blog/2007/03/fairy-use-tale

Fatma Er, N., & Er, M. (2016). The effects of student-content interaction on academic performance in distance-learning courses. *International Journal on New Trends in Education and Their Implications, 7*(3), 60–68. https://www.researchgate.net/publication/329874133

Flores, N., & Rosa, J. (2015). Undoing appropriateness: Raciolinguistic ideologies and language diversity in education. *Harvard Educational Review, 85*(2), 149–171. https://doi.org/10.17763/0017-8055.85.2.149

Fuller, M. (2017). An update on the Family Educational Rights and Privacy Act. *New Directions for Institutional Research, 2016*(172), 25–36. https://doi.org/10.1002/ir.20201

Garrison, D. R., Anderson, T., & Archer, W. (1999). Critical inquiry in a text-based environment: Computer conferencing in higher education. *The Internet and Higher Education, 2*(2–3), 87–105. https://doi.org/10.1016/S1096-7516(00)00016-6.

Gaytan, J. (2013). Factors affecting student retention in online courses: Overcoming this critical problem. *Career and Technical Education Research, 38*(2), 145–155. https://doi.org/10.5328/cter38.2.147

Globokar, J. L. (2012). *Introduction to online learning: A guide for students.* SAGE Publications.

Graff, N. (2011). "An effective and agonizing way to learn": Backwards design and new teachers' preparation for planning curriculum. *Teacher Education Quarterly, 38*(3), 151–168. https://www.jstor.org/stable/23479622

Grillo, M. C., & Leist, C. W. (2013). Academic support as a predictor of retention to graduation: New insights on the role of tutoring, learning assistance, and supplemental instruction. *Journal of College Student Retention: Research, Theory and Practice, 15*(3), 387–408. https://doi.org/10.2190/CS.15.3.e

Grosz, E. (1994). *Volatile bodies: Toward a corporeal feminism.* Indiana University Press.

Herbert, M. (2006). Staying the course: A study in online student satisfaction and retention. *Online Journal of Distance Learning Administration, 9*(4). http://www.westga.edu/~distance/ojdla/winter94/herbert94.htm

Hintze, M. (2017). In defense of the long privacy statement. *Maryland Law Review, 76*(4), 1044–1085. https://ssrn.com/abstract=2910583

Howard, S. K., Ma, J., & Yang, J. (2016). Student rules: Exploring patterns of students' computer-efficacy and engagement with digital technologies in learning. *Computers & Education, 101*, 29–42. https://doi.org/10.1016/j.compedu.2016.05.008

Inoue, A. B. (2015). *Antiracist writing assessment ecologies: Teaching and assessing writing for a socially just future*. The WAC Clearinghouse; Parlor Press.

Inoue, A. B. (2017). *Antiracist writing pedagogy: Racialized places of labor and listening*. Studies in Writing and Rhetoric. https://swreditors.org/antiracist-writing-pedagogy-racialized-places-of-labor-and-listening/#more-805

Inoue, A. B. (2019). *Labor-based grading contracts: Building equity and inclusion in the compassionate writing classroom*. The WAC Clearinghouse; University Press of Colorado.

Jenkins, H., Clinton, K., Purushotma, R., Robison, A. J., & Weigel, M. (2006). *Confronting the challenges of participatory culture: Media education for the 21st century*. MacArthur Foundation. https://www.macfound.org/media/article_pdfs/jenkins_white_paper.pdf

Joksimovic, S., Gasevic, D., Kovanovic. V., Riecke, B.E., & Hatala, M. (2015). Social presence in online discussions as a process predictor of academic performance. *Journal of Computer Assisted Learning, 31*(6), 638–654. https://doi.org/10.1111/jcal.12107

Kamenetz, A. (2010). *DIY U: Edupunks, edupreneurs, and the coming transformation of higher education*. Chelsea Green Publishing.

Kryger, K., & Zimmerman, G. X. (2020). Neurodivergence and intersectionality in labor-based grading contracts. *Journal of Writing Assessment, 13*(2). https://escholarship.org/content/qt0934x4rm/qt0934x4rm.pdf?t=r07b8o

Lehman, R. M., & Conceição, S. C. O. (2010). *Creating a sense of presence in online teaching: How to "be there" for distance learners*. Jossey-Bass.

Levine, R. (1997). *A geography of time: The temporal misadventures of a social psychologist, or how every culture keeps time just a little bit differently* (1st ed.). Basic Books.

Lewis, S., Whiteside, A., & Garrett Dikkers, A. (2014). Autonomy and responsibility: Online learning as a solution for at-risk high school students. *International Journal of E-Learning & Distance Education, 29*(2). http://www.ijede.ca/index.php/jde/article/view/883

Linder, K. E. (2017). *The blended course design workbook: A practical guide*. Stylus Publishing.

Lindh, M., & Nolin, J. (2016). Information we collect: Surveillance and privacy in the implementation of Google Apps for Education. *European Educational Research Journal, 15*(6), 1–20. https://doi.org/10.1177/1474904116654917

Markel, M. (2005). The rhetoric of misdirection in corporate privacy-policy statements. *Technical Communication Quarterly, 14*(2), 197–214. https://doi.org/10.1207/s15427625tcq1402_5

Matuga, J. M. (2009). Self-regulation, goal orientation, and academic achievement of secondary students in online university courses. *Educational Technology & Society, 12*(3), 4–11. https://www.jstor.org/stable/jeductechsoci.12.3.4

Mayer, R. E. (2020). *Multimedia learning* (3rd ed.). Cambridge University Press.

Meyer, K., Bruwelheide, J., & Poulin, R. (2009). Why they stayed: Near-perfect retention in an online certification program in library media. *Journal of Asynchronous Learning Networks, 13*(3), 129–145. http://doi.org/10.24059/olj.v10i4.1747

Mitchum, C., Hebbard, M., & Morris, J. (2021). Expanding instructional contexts: Why student backgrounds matter to online teaching and learning. In W. Banks & S. Spangler (Eds.), *English studies online: Programs, practices, possibilities*. Parlor Press.

Moore, K., Bartkovich, J., Fetzner, M., & Ison, S. (2003). Success in cyberspace: Student retention in online courses. *Journal of Applied Research in the Community College, 10*(2), 107–118. https://www.learntechlib.org/p/104016/

Moore, M. (1989). Editorial: Three types of interaction. *The American Journal of Distance Education, 3*(2), 1–7. https://doi.org/10.1080/08923648909526659

Moore, M. (2019). The theory of transactional distance. In M. Moore & W. Diehl (Eds.), *Handbook of distance education* (4th ed.). (pp. 32–46). Routledge.

Moran, K. (2020, April 5). *How people read online: New and old findings.*

Morris, L. V., & Finnegan, C. L. (2008). Best practices in predicting and encouraging student persistence and achievement online. *Journal of College Student Retention: Research, Theory & Practice, 10*(1), 55–64. https://doi.org/10.2190/CS.10.1.e

Nash, R. D. (2005). Course completion rates among distance learners: Identifying possible methods to improve retention. *Online Journal of Distance Learning Administration, 8*(4). http://www.westga.edu/~distance/ojdla/winter84/nash84.htm

National Council of Teachers of English. (2008). *The NCTE definition of 21st century literacies*. http://www.ncte.org/positions/statements/21stcentdefinition

National Council of Teachers of English. (2018). *Beliefs for integrating technology into the English language arts classroom*. https://ncte.org/statement/beliefs-technology-preparation-english-teachers/

National Council of Teachers of English. (2019). *Definition of literacy in a digital age*. https://ncte.org/statement/nctes-definition-literacy-digital-age/

Newmann, F. M., Wehlage, G. G., & Lamborn, S. D. (1992). The significance and sources of student engagement. In F. M. Newmann (Ed.), *Student engagement and achievement in American secondary schools* (pp. 11–39). Teachers College Press.

Nichols, M. (2010). Student perceptions of support services and the influence of targeted interventions on retention in distance education. *Distance Education, 31*(1), 93–113. https://doi.org/10.1080/01587911003725048

Nielsen Norman Group. https://www.nngroup.com/articles/how-people-read-online/

Nilson, L. B. (2014). *Specifications grading: Restoring rigor, motivating students, and saving faculty time*. Stylus Publishing.

Nilson, L. B. (2016). *Teaching at its best: A research-based resource for college instructors* (4th ed.). Jossey-Bass.

Nilson, L. B., & Goodson, L. A. (2017). *Online teaching at its best: Merging instructional design with teaching and learning research*. Jossey-Bass.

Novak, K., & Thibodeau, T. (2016). *UDL in the cloud! How to design and deliver online education using Universal Design for Learning*. CAST Professional Publishing.

Parkes, J., & Zimmaro, D. (2017). *The college classroom assessment compendium : A practical guide to the college instructor's daily assessment life* [eBook edition]. ProQuest Ebook Central. https://ebookcentral.proquest.com

Partnership for 21st Century Skills. (2019) *Framework for 21st century learning*. https://static.battelleforkids.org/documents/p21/P21_Framework_Brief.pdf

Peacock, S., & Cowan, J. (2019). Promoting sense of belonging in online learning communities of inquiry in accredited courses. *Online Learning, 23*(2), 67–81. https://doi.org/10.24059/olj.v23i2.1488

Phirangee, K., Epp, C. D., & Hewitt, J. (2016). Exploring the relationships between facilitation methods, students' sense of community, and their online behaviors. *Online Learning, 20*(2). http://doi.org/10.24059/olj.v20i2.775

Pike, G. R., Kuh, G. D., & McCormick, A. C. (2011). An investigation of the contingent relationships between learning community participation and student engagement. *Research in Higher Education, 52*(3), 300–322. https://doi.org/10.1007/s11162-010-9192-1

Pleitz, J. D., MacDougall, A. E., Terry, R. A., Buckley, M. R., & Campbell, N. J. (2015). Great expectations: Examining the discrepancy between expectations and experiences on college student retention. *Journal of College Student Retention: Research, Theory & Practice, 17*(1), 88–104. https://doi.org/10.1177/1521025115571252

Pontes, M. C. F., Hasit, C., Pontes, N. M. H., Lewis, P. A., & Siefring, K. T. (2010). Variables related to undergraduate students preference for distance education classes. *Online Journal of Distance Learning Administration, 13*(2). https://ojdla.com/archive/summer132/pontes_pontes132.pdf

Price, M. (2011). *Mad at school: Rhetorics of mental disability and academic life*. University of Michigan Press. https://doi.org/10.3998/mpub.1612837

Purdy, J. P. (2010). The changing space of research: Web 2.0 and the integration of research and writing environments. *Computers and Composition, 27*(1), 48–58. https://doi.org/10.1016/j.compcom.2009.12.001

Quality Matters. (2018). *Quality matters higher education rubric* (6th ed). Maryland Online Inc.

Rehabilitation Act of 1973, Section 504, 29 U.S.C. §701 *et seq*. (1973). https://www.law.cornell.edu/uscode/text/29/701

Reiser, R. A., & Dempsey, J. V. (2018). *Trends and issues in instructional design and technology* (4th ed.). Pearson.

Richardson, J. C., Maeda, Y., Lv, J., & Caskurlu, S. (2017). Social presence in relation to students' satisfaction and learning in the online environment: A meta-analysis. *Computers in Human Behavior, 71*, 402–417. http://doi.org/10.1016/j.chb.2017.02.001

Richlin, L. (2006). *Blueprint for learning: Constructing college courses to facilitate, assess, and document learning*. Stylus Publishing.

Roberts, J., & Styron, R. (2006). Student satisfaction and persistence: Factors vital to student retention. *Research in Higher Education Journal, 6*, 1–18. http://www.aabri.com/manuscripts/09321.pdf

Rodrigo, R. (2013). Can you Digg it?: Using web applications in teaching the research process. *The Journal of Interactive Technology and Pedagogy,* 4. http://jitp.commons.gc.cuny.edu/can-you-digg-it-using-web-applications-in-teaching-the-research-process/.

Rogers, P., & Lea, M. (2005). Social presence in distributed group environments: The role of social identity. *Behaviour & Information Technology, 24*(2), 151–158. https://doi.org/10.1080/01449290410001723472

Rourke, L., Anderson, T., Garrison, D. R., & Archer, W. (1999). Assessing social presence in asynchronous text-based computer conferencing. *The Journal of Distance Education, 14*(2), 51–70. https://www.learntechlib.org/p/92000/

Sadeghi, S., Wittmann, M., De Rosa, E., & Anderson, A. K. (2023). Wrinkles in subsecond time perception are synchronized to the heart. *Psychophysiology, 60*(8). https://doi.org/10.1111/psyp.14270

Saldaña, J. (2021). *The coding manual for qualitative researchers* (4th ed.). SAGE Publications.

Saleh, A., & Danish, J. (2018). Zone of proximal development. In B. Frey (Ed.), *The SAGE encyclopedia of educational research, measurement, and evaluation* (pp. 1839–1841). *SAGE knowledge.* http://dx.doi.org/10.4135/9781506326139.n757

Schmidt, P. S., & Kruger-Ross, M. J. (2022). *Reimagining literacies in the digital age: Multimodal strategies to teach with technology*. National Council of Teachers of English.

Selwyn, N. (2009). The digital native—myth and reality. *Aslib Proceedings, 61*(4), 364–379. https://doi.org/10.1108/00012530910973776

Shea, P., Li, C. S., & Pickett, A. (2006). A study of teaching presence and student sense of learning community in fully online and web-enhanced college courses. *The Internet and Higher Education, 9*(3), 175–190. https://doi.org/10.1016/j.iheduc.2006.06.005

Smith, L. T. (2012). *Decolonizing methodologies: Research and indigenous peoples* (2nd ed.). Zed Books.

Song, L., Singleton, E. S., Hill, J. R., & Koh, M. H. (2004). Improving online learning: Student perceptions of useful and challenging characteristics. *The Internet and Higher Education*, *7*(1), 59–70. https://doi.org/10.1016/j.iheduc.2003.11.003

Sorapure, M. (2010). Information visualization, web 2.0, and the teaching of writing. *Computers and Composition, 27*(1), 59–70. https://doi.org/10.1016/j.compcom.2009.12.003

Stewart, M. K., Hilliard, L., Stillman-Webb, N., & Cunningham, J. M. (2021). The community of inquiry in writing studies survey: Interpreting social presence in disciplinary contexts. *Online Learning, 25*(2), 73–94. https://doi.org/10.24059/olj.v25i2.2275

Stranach, M. (2017). *Social presence in two massive open online courses (MOOCs): A multiple case study* [Unpublished doctoral dissertation]. University of Calgary.

Sumeeth, M., Singh, R. I., & Miller, J. (2010). Are online privacy policies readable? *International Journal of Information Security and Privacy, 4*(1), 93–116. https://doi.org/10.4018/jisp.2010010105

Swan, K., & Shih, L. F. (2005). On the nature and development of social presence in online course discussions. *Journal of Asynchronous Learning Networks, 9*(3), 115–136. http://doi.org/10.24059/olj.v9i3.1788

Taie, S., & Goldring, R. (2019). *Characteristics of public and private elementary and secondary schools in the United States: Results from the 2017–18 National Teacher and Principal Survey*. U.S. Department of Education. National Center for Education Statistics. https://nces.ed.gov/pubsearch/pubsinfo.asp?pubid=2019140

Tinto, V. (1975). Dropout from higher education: A theoretical synthesis of recent research. *Review of Educational Research, 45*(1), 89–125. https://doi.org/10.3102/00346543045001089

Tschantz, M. C., Datta, A., & Wing, J. M. (2012). *Formalizing and enforcing purpose restrictions in privacy policies*. 2012 IEEE Symposium on Security and Privacy, San Francisco, CA. https://doi.org/10.1109/SP.2012.21

U.S. Copyright Act, 17 U.S.C. §§ 101-810 (2021). https://www.copyright.gov/title17/

U.S. Department of Education. (2021a). *Family Educational Rights and Privacy Act (FERPA)*. https://www2.ed.gov/policy/gen/guid/fpco/ferpa/index.html

U.S. Department of Education. (2021b). *Percent of students enrolled in distance education courses* [Infographic]. IES>NCES. https://nces.ed.gov/ipeds/TrendGenerator/app/answer/2/42

van der Meer, J., Jansen, E., & Torenbeek, M. (2010). 'It's almost a mindset that teachers need to change': First-year students' need to be inducted into time management. *Studies in Higher Education, 35*(7), 777–791. https://doi.org/10.1080/03075070903383211

Wandler, J., & Imbriale, W. J. (2017). Promoting college student self-regulation in online learning environments. *Online Learning, 21*(2). https://doi.org/10.24059/olj.v21i2.881

Whiteside, A. L. (2015). Introducing the social presence model to explore online and blended learning experiences. *Online Learning, 19*(2), 1–20. http://doi.org/10.24059/olj.v19i2.453

Wiggins, G., & McTighe, J. (2005). *Understanding by design* (expanded 2nd ed.). Association for Supervision and Curriculum Development.

Wittmann, M. (2017). *Felt time: The science of how we experience time* (E. Butler, Trans.). The MIT Press. (Original work published 2014)

Womack, A. (2017). Teaching is accommodation: Universally designing composition classrooms and syllabi. *College Composition and Communication, 68*(3), 494–525. http://www.ncte.org/library/NCTEFiles/Resources/Journals/CCC/0683-feb2017/CCCC0683Teaching.pdf

Wood, T. (2017). Cripping time in the college composition classroom. *College Composition and Communication, 69*(2), 260–286. https://prod-ncte-cdn.azureedge.net/nctefiles/resources/journals/ccc/0692-dec2017/ccc0692cripping.pdf

Yancey, K. B. (1998). *Reflection in the writing classroom*. Utah State University Press.

Young, V. A. (2009). "Nah, we straight": An argument against code switching. *JAC, 29*(1/2), 49–76.

Index

Note: A 't' following a page number indicates a table; an 'f' indicates a figure.

Authors

Rochelle (Shelley) Rodrigo is the Senior Director of the Writing Program; professor in the Rhetoric, Composition, and the Teaching of English (RCTE) program; writing scholar (continuing status) in the Department of English; and affiliate faculty with the School of Information at the University of Arizona. She researches how "newer" technologies better facilitate communicative interactions, specifically teaching and learning. As well as coauthoring three editions of *The Wadsworth/Cengage Guide to Research*, she also coedited *Rhetorically Rethinking Usability* (Hampton Press). Her scholarly work has appeared in journals such as *Composition Forum, Composition Studies, Computers and Composition, C&C Online, Technical Communication Quarterly, Teaching English in the Two-Year College*, as well as various edited collections. In 2022, she became a research associate with The Readability Consortium and a distinguished fellow in the Center for University Education Scholarship (CUES) at the University of Arizona. In 2021, she was elected vice president (four-year term including president) of the National Council of Teachers of English and won the Arizona Technology in Education Association's Ruth Catalano Friend of Technology Innovation Award. In 2018, she became an Adobe Education Leader. In 2014, she was awarded Old Dominion University's annual Teaching with Technology Award. In 2012, she received the Digital Humanities High Powered Computing Fellowship. And, in 2010, she became a Google Certified Teacher/Innovator.

Dr. Catrina Mitchum is adjuncting as an associate professor with University of Maryland Global Campus. She has been designing and teaching online learning experiences since 2009. She has been awarded various teaching awards, including one in Professional and Technical Writing and one for Collaborative Teaching. She has taught first-year writing courses, upper-level undergraduate courses in Professional and Technical Writing, and introduction to research courses, entirely online. Her research interests are in retention, design, and delivery of online writing classes, and teaching with technology. She has scholarly work published in *Currents in Teaching and Learning*, *Composition Forum*, and *The Journal of Teaching and Learning with Technology*, among other journals and edited collections. She was awarded, with other scholars, the CCCC Research Initiative Grant in 2018 and a Digital Learning Tech Seed Grant in 2021, and in 2021–2022, she was an Inclusive Leadership Fellow.

This book was typeset in AvenirNext, Myriad Pro, and Palatino by Barbara Frazier.

The typefaces used on the cover include Cera Pro.

The book was printed on 50 lb., white offset paper.